THE DEPTHS OF LIFE

MERCER UNIVERSITY

MERCER UNIVERSITY PRESS

Endowed by

TOM WATSON BROWN

and

THE WATSON-BROWN FOUNDATION, INC.

THE DEPTHS OF LIFE

Paul Tillich's Understanding of God

Duane Olson

MERCER UNIVERSITY PRESS
Macon, Georgia
1979–2019
40 Years of Publishing Excellence

MUP/ P594

Published by Mercer University Press
1501 Mercer University Drive
Macon, Georgia 31207

9 8 7 6 5 4 3 2 1

Books published by Mercer University Press are printed on acid-free paper that meets the requirements of the American National Standard for Information Sciences—Permanence of Paper for Printed Library Materials.

Printed and bound in the United States.

This book is set in Adobe Caslon Pro.

Cover/jacket design by Burt&Burt

ISBN 978-0-88146-726-0
Cataloging-in-Publication Data is available from the Library of Congress

CONTENTS

This book is dedicated to my wife Brenda,
with gratefulness for being included in your rich embrace of life.

Abbreviations

WORKS BY PAUL TILLICH

CB – *The Courage to Be*. New Haven and London: Yale University Press, 1952.

CE – *Christianity and the Encounter of the World Religions*. New York: Columbia University Press, 1963.

DF - *Dynamics of Faith*. New York: Harper and Row, 1957.

FR – *The Future of Religions*. New York: Harper and Row, 1966.

PR – *Philosophy of Religion*, in *What is Religion?*. New York, Evanston, and London: Harper and Row, 1969.

PE – *The Protestant Era*, abridged edition. Chicago: University of Chicago Press, 1957.

SS – *System of the Sciences according to Objects and Methods*. London and Toronto: Associated University Presses, 1981

ST I,II,III – *Systematic Theology*. Chicago: University of Chicago Press, 1951, 1957, 1963.

TC – *Theology of Culture*. London, Oxford, New York: Oxford University Press, 1959.

Acknowledgments

I am grateful for the sabbatical I received from McKendree University that allowed me the opportunity to write this book, and I give a special thanks to my colleagues at McKendree with whom I enjoy a vibrant, ongoing, intellectual relationship.

My interest in Paul Tillich goes back to my undergraduate days at Trinity College where I was introduced to Tillich in a philosophy of religion class taught by Dr. David Schlafer. At Princeton Theological Seminary, I took my first semester-long class on Tillich with Dr. Mark Lewis Taylor. All of the students who took that class over the years know how rich, insightful, and expertly crafted it was. It was in my PhD program at the University of Iowa under the tutelage of Dr. David Klemm, however, where my appreciation for Tillich's thought fully flowered. *Dynamics of Faith* was a required text in a large undergraduate course taught by Professor Klemm where I served as one of several Teaching Assistants. Over the course of several semesters, I heard Professor Klemm again and again expertly explain Tillich's idea of God and God's relation to the world in a nuanced, compelling, and relevant way. The inspiration from Dr Klemm's deep insight into the meaning of Tillich's thought was the main motivation for pursuing my dissertation on Tillich under his guidance.

Late in my graduate school career, at a conference, I was introduced to the North American Paul Tillich Society, a professional organization committed to the study of Tillich's thought. From my first meeting of the conference, I recognized how valuable this organization was for its unyielding analysis of the depth, breadth, and ongoing relevance of Tillich's ideas. For more than twenty-five years I have been involved in the Society, serving on the Board of Directors several times and as its President. Words fail me in attempting to express my gratitude to its skilled and knowledgeable members. Through the Society, I have had the privilege of getting to know a host of scholars with expertise on Tillich, a number of whom not only know Tillich's work, but were students of Tillich himself. Being involved in the North American Paul Tillich Society has shown me that scholars across the country continue to see Tillich's thought as valuable and use it in analyzing the contemporary situation in a myriad of ways. Through the North American Paul Tillich Society, I have also had the privilege of knowing and learning from members of the German and French-speaking Paul Tillich Society. Indeed, scholarship on Tillich continues to be rich and vital. I ride on a wave produced by a multitude.

On a personal note, my wife Brenda continues to be an inspiration. Sharing in her love of film, literature, art, music, travel, nature, gardening, people, and events makes my life rich and rewarding. Her insights into life, politics, people, and the global context in which we live, continues to challenge and broaden me.

Introduction
God and the Universe

Gazing at the stars in the night sky, ancient people certainly understood that the universe was vast. It has only been in the modern period, however, that we have been progressively led to understand just how vast it is. The most recent stages of this story are compelling. As late as the first decades of the twentieth century, astronomers debated whether the gaseous clouds they saw in the night sky were within our Milky Way galaxy or beyond it. It was only in 1929 that Edwin Hubble, creatively piecing together the evidence, published a paper showing the gaseous clouds were in fact galaxies that lay beyond our own. [1]

Today, we live with the commonplace knowledge that there are multitudes of galaxies. Everywhere the Hubble telescope looks, even to what were previously thought to be dark spots in space, it finds galaxies. Just how many there are continues to be studied, although such studies are done with the understanding that we must speak about the number of galaxies in the observable universe rather than the universe as a whole. Travelling at 186,000 miles per second, light is fast, but it seems slow in relation to the

---

[1] "1923: Other Galaxies Exist," *Amazing Space: Space Telescope Education Program,* https://amazing-space.stsci.edu/resources/explorations/groundup/lesson/scopes/mt_wilson/discovery.php.

vast reaches of space. The nearest galaxy to our Milky Way is more than two million light years away. What we observe in that galaxy through our telescopes took place that long ago. In the case of far distant galaxies, light has been travelling for billions of years to reach us. While looking into the distance means looking back in time, we can never see further than the universe is old, the maximum length of time light could have travelled to reach us. The current estimate of the age of the universe is between 13-14 billion years. Piecing together observations from the Hubble telescope, the number of galaxies in the observable universe has been estimated at between 100 and 200 billion, each with hundreds of millions of stars, although there may be many times more than that.[2]

This is our universe. In relation to it, the universe of the biblical writers seems positively quaint. In the creation story of Genesis, on day two, God separates the waters below from the waters above by putting in place the hard dome of the sky (Gen. 1:6-8). On day four, God places the "greater light" and the "lesser light," the sun and the moon, along with the stars into the dome. They separate day from night, discriminating seasons and years, and also serving as signs (Gen 1:14-19). The vast reaches of space are brought close, as the sun, moon, and stars equally circle the earth in a purposive way.

In the worldview of the Hebrew Bible, the place of God's dwelling is in the heavens above the dome (e.g. Ps 103:19, 123:1). In the image of the royal monarch, God is seated on a heavenly throne surrounded by the hosts of heaven who are envisioned in a

---

[2] Elizabeth Howell, "How Many Galaxies Are There?" April 1 2014, http://www.space.com/25303-how-many-galaxies-are-in-the-universe.html.

variety of ways as winged creatures or angelic beings (I Kgs 22:19-23, Isa. 6:1-6).[3]

With some modifications, this cosmology continues into the New Testament period. Foreign astrologers see the sign of the birth of the Messiah in an appearing star (Matt. 2:2), while an angel appears to announce the birth to shepherds, and, with the heavenly hosts, praises God in the highest heaven before returning there (Lk 2:8-15). A dove descends and a Divine voice speaks to Jesus from heaven at his baptism (Mk 1:9-11), and during his ministry (Jn 12:28). Jesus teaches his followers to pray to their father in heaven, and is often portrayed looking up to God as he prays. In the Gospel of John, Jesus describes himself as having "come down from heaven" to do God's will (Jn 6:38). Predicting the end of time, he says earthquakes will portend it, and, following the prophets, it will involve the darkening of the sun and the moon with the "stars...falling from heaven," after which the Son of Man will appear in the clouds, send out his angels, and gather the elect (Mk 13:8, 24-27).

The Christian theology that develops around Jesus is expressed in this worldview. In the most important creed of the Christian church, the Nicene Creed, Jesus Christ, who shares the being of God, is said to have "come down from heaven," becoming incarnate in a virgin. Following his atoning death, according to the creed, Jesus "rose" and "ascended into heaven where he is seated at the right hand of the father from whence he shall come to judge the living and the dead." The developing liturgy of the church echoes this descent and ascent of the savior to God's right hand, and anticipates Jesus' return from his heavenly location.

---

[3] For a detailed summary of the biblical cosmology see J. Edward Wright, "Cosmogony, Cosmology," in *The New Interpreters Dictionary of the Bible,* vol. 1 (Nashville: Abingdon Press, 2006) 758-761.

Our universe is vast and ancient. Comparatively speaking, the biblical universe was understood to be small and young. In our universe, there is no hard dome or edge above which the deity dwells, interacting with our world in a descending and ascending way. One of the major questions of Christian theology over the last 100 years or so has been whether we need to change the way we think about God and God's relationship to the universe to account for the differences between the biblical worldview or cosmology and our own.[4]

One of the most intriguing texts to engage this question is a slim volume of theology published in 1963 by the Anglican Bishop John Robinson titled, *Honest to God*. Fairly quickly after its publication, the book was translated into more than seventeen languages and went on to sell more than a million copies. Over the years, the book has maintained a significant level of popularity, provoking conferences and other events commemorating the 25th, 40th, and 50th anniversaries of its publication.[5]

Robinson makes the claim that the Christian idea of God has already undergone change in the past few centuries. Even the most sophisticated biblical theologians, a designation Robinson accords John and Paul, could write of God being "up there" or in heaven above us in an immediate and literal way that required no caveats or explanations.[6] Modern advances in our understanding of the universe from Copernicus forward have made it impossible to continue holding that view. To Robinson, with a new cosmology, our

---

[4] The question whether we need to change our thinking about God is not only due to a different cosmology between the contemporary and biblical worldview but to other intellectual developments from modernity forward. They are discussed throughout the text.

[5] "Honest to God: Introduction," *Modern Church: Liberal Faith in a Changing World,* http://modernchurch.org.uk/honest-to-god.

[6] John A.T. Robinson, *Honest to God* (Philadelphia: Westminster Press, 1963) 11-12.

understanding of God developed. God was no longer literally "up there," but "out there."[7] God was not localized in a specific space above our heads, but God was still conceptualized as an independent being alongside the universe. God was a definite thing or person, someone out there watching the events of history go by and free to intervene in history from time to time as God saw fit.

For Robinson, the sea change required in the contemporary period is that even the God "out there" has to go, or, better put, this idea of God needs to be translated into something else.[8] A God "out there," or, a God alongside the universe, is still primarily conceived in terms of a spatial relationship with the world. And while "up" has been changed to "out," we know there is literally no edge "out there" beyond which God exists. So what do we mean when we use traditional language suggesting God is "out there?" If we cannot answer this, or make an easy mental shift to a different idea of God, then, thought Robinson, Christianity would seem increasingly irrelevant or even outlandish.

It was primarily to the work of Paul Tillich (1886-1965) that Robinson turned to expound an alternative understanding of God and God's relationship to the universe.[9] When Robinson wrote his book, Tillich was still actively working and had not yet published the third and final volume of his groundbreaking *Systematic Theology*. Tillich was an apt choice, since more than any other Protestant theologian of the mid-twentieth century, it was Tillich who argued vehemently of the need for a new idea of God that both fit the contemporary understanding of the world and was adequate to what we mean when we speak of God. Tillich had, in his own way, rocked the English speaking Protestant world, or at

---

[7] Robinson, *Honest to God*, 13.

[8] Robinson, *Honest to God*, 14-18.

[9] Robinson also analyzes the work of Rudolph Bultmann and some suggestive late writings of Dietrich Bonhoeffer, but for the basic metaphysical reconstruction he proposes, he relies on Tillich.

least a certain part of it interested in Christian theology, when, in 1951, he published the first volume of his *Systematic Theology*. In this volume he declared vehemently that "God does not exist," "God is…not a being," and "[t]he being of God cannot be understood as the existence of a being alongside others or above others."[10] What could a Christian theologian possibly mean when he says God does not exist and God is not a being alongside the universe? What is the alternative understanding of God into which we are to translate the old language of God as "up there," or "out there"? These questions were central to Tillich's thought, and more than any other theologian of his generation, he sought to answer them in a thoroughgoing and systematic way.

It is the thesis of this book that these questions remain relevant, and that Tillich's understanding of God and God's relationship to the universe provides the best platform for articulating a response to them. For Tillich, God is neither "up there" nor "out there." God is "through here." God is in the depths of life. Explicating what that means through a sophisticated grasp of reality that accounts for the history of Western philosophical and theological reflection was, arguably, Tillich's central intellectual task. What he accomplished was groundbreaking precisely because his achievement was united with what came before even while he effectively translated it into something new and relevant for the contemporary world.

Robinson himself hypothesized it would take generations to make the translation from a God "out there" to another idea of God.[11] For his own part, as enticing and insightful as it is, there is a kind of tentativeness and suggestiveness in Robinson's analysis of Tillich. He quotes from Tillich's theological works, and also

---

[10] *ST* 1 205, 237, 235.

[11] Robinson, *Honest to God*, 15.

from his sermons and popular writings. In Robinson's text, certainly the framework of what Tillich intended comes through. And yet the work remains more suggestive than definitive.

The decades since Robinson's time have witnessed rounds of scholarly analysis on Tillich and his work. The groundbreaking character of his achievement has been affirmed by many, even by those who disagree with his conclusions. Ambiguities in his thought have been clarified and implications teased out. Questions have been analyzed about just what his thought means given cultural changes since his time such as the women's movement, the environmental movement, globalization and the increased interaction of representatives of the world religions, the push for LGBT rights, and a host of intellectual developments, trends, and thinkers that separate 1965 from our own day. Through it all, Tillich's work has continued to be acknowledged as important. And yet, while important, it remains difficult to access.

Tillich's writings are dense. His most important English work, the *Systematic Theology*, consists of three volumes and approximately 900 pages. The book is the translation into narrative form of lectures from his graduate school classes. The lectures themselves originally consisted of theses that he would read and then expound upon verbally. Tillich was a systematizer. Every idea was connected to every other idea and to say one thing required showing its relationship to the whole, which was always greater than the sum of its parts. Every idea has a history. Almost always, when Tillich expounded on an idea or a position he was taking, he did it in relationship to the history of important thinkers vis-à-vis this idea. Commonly, he would run through names and generations of thinkers at breakneck speed, although the text of his *Systematic Theology* is almost entirely devoid of citations.

Tillich wrote popular single-issue texts and was a renowned lecturer in his time. Many of those texts continue to be read and studied, including important texts on faith (*Dynamics of Faith*), courage *(The Courage to Be)*, and ethics (*Love, Power, and Justice*). However, Tillich wrote no popular single-issue text on God. This most central idea in his thought remains infused throughout the totality of his thought.

As someone who has spent a career teaching religious studies at the undergraduate level, and someone who is deeply influenced by Tillich's thought, I have experienced the struggle to convey Tillich's understanding of God to undergraduate students. While it is absolutely central to his thought, it is slippery and confounding to grasp. How can we understand who God is if God does not exist and God is not a being alongside the universe? What does this alternative understanding of God mean? On an individual level, this book emerges from that difficulty. It is my hope that Tillich's understanding of God and its major implications for religious studies and cultural life is portrayed in a way that can be grasped by students and anyone curious about thinking through Tillich's alternative framework for God.

Because I have wanted to present Tillich's ideas with the least amount of technical language possible, I have, for the most part, avoided extensive quotes from his work in the text. Many suggestions for further implications of his thinking, and secondary sources on his work, have been put in the footnotes. I have done my best to state things in my own way. Tillich developed a distinctive vocabulary that is very powerful but also can be off-putting for some. Certainly some of his vocabulary cannot be avoided, but in an attempt at clarity, I have tried to use more colloquial than technical language. At times, in an attempt to make Tillich's position clear, I expand on or develop arguments he makes. There are other times when I make arguments Tillich never explicitly made (as far as I know), but that emerge as implications of his thought. I realize this means that despite my best efforts to be clear about the distinction, there are times in the text where it may be difficult to tell where Tillich's thought ends and my explanations begin. I only hope that readers wanting to grasp that line more clearly will be moved to examine Tillich's own texts.

The greatest challenge in presenting Tillich's understanding of God has been deciding what to leave out. Tillich's understanding of God is at the heart of his thought. As such, it is connected with everything else he said. I have struggled to know how to present this central contention adequately without presenting everything else. This problem is no doubt inevitable when dealing with a thinker of Tillich's stature. I alone am responsible for the judgment about what is left out in this presentation of Tillich's understanding of God. Tillich scholars will know that what is left out is considerable and debatable. Once again, for those being introduced to Tillich for the first time, it is my hope this text will turn them to Tillich's own work for deeper and more extensive connections.

Why a Book on Tillich's Understanding of God?

This book argues that Tillich's understanding of God is important and relevant in the contemporary context. One of the reasons for its relevance lies in a recent development that neither Robinson nor Tillich could have foreseen. It has to do with the number of people in the contemporary period in the US who are unaffiliating from religious traditions. In religious scholarship, these people are called the "nones."

While some of the nones are atheist or agnostic, the majority of them are not.[12] They believe something when it comes to religion or spirituality. The concrete content of their beliefs may vary significantly from person to person. What unites the nones is not

[12] According to the Pew Forum, 33% are atheist and 6% agnostic. *Religious Landscape Study*, 2014, http://www.pewforum.org/religious-landscape-study/religious-tradition/unaffiliated-religious-nones/.

what they do or do not believe. It is what they do not do. They do not affiliate with any Christian denomination or other world religion.

The Pew Forum does the most extensive polls we have on US citizens's religious beliefs, including extensive nation-wide polls done in 2007 and 2014. The group experiencing the greatest growth in those seven years were the nones. They grew from 16.1% to 22.8% of the population.[13] That means, accounting for a margin of error that can be off a few million in either direction, 21 or so million Americans were added to a group that now contains approximately 73 million Americans. There are more nones than mainline Protestants. There are more nones than Roman Catholics.

One of the reasons the nones are growing is because the younger population is much more likely to take this position. Well more than a third of those who are 18-49 are nones. For those more than 65, the total is 9%. If this trend continues, as the younger generation replaces the older, the number of nones will continue to grow.

The explosive growth of the nones comes at the very time evangelical Protestantism has shown its first decline in decades. Tillich and Robinson, working in the 1950s and 60s, were both concerned that if Christianity did not square its ideas with the modern world, it would lose its viability. Both were critical of elements of evangelical Protestantism in this regard. Yet evangelical Protestants grew vigorously from the 1960's forward, while mainline Protestants, those groups notable for having a wing that is open to new ideas, shrank precipitously. That shrinking continues,

---

13 *America's Changing Religious* Landscape, May 12, 2015, http://www.pewforum.org/2015/05/12/americas-changing-religious-landscape/.

going from 18.1% to 14.7% between 2007 and 2014. The shrinking has hit the Roman Catholic Church, with its strong intellectual traditions, as well. Despite the continued influx of Roman Catholic immigrants, the percentage of Americans identifying as Catholic dropped from 23.9% to 20.8%.

While Tillich certainly could not have anticipated these trends, there is within his thought the capacity to respond to them. While the rise of the nones comes from a variety of sources, one can reasonably hypothesize that contained within the 21 million new nones, there must be a multitude of religious questions and even crises. There must be people who say, "I just cannot believe what I used to believe because the old beliefs no longer make sense to me." Tillich's thought was constructed to address that struggle. His goal always was to formulate or reformulate beliefs in response to the questions of the modern period in a way that shows religious ideas and, for him, Christian beliefs can be compatible with contemporary thinking. Central to that formulation or reformulation is Tillich's distinctive understanding of God and God's relation to the universe.

As to other groups of nones, like the avowed atheists or the cultured despisers of religion, Tillich's thought was directed to them as well.[14] He constantly told those who said they did not

[14] The reference to the "cultured despisers" of religion is from a 1799 text by the German theologian Friedrich Schleiermacher called, *On Religion: Speeches to its Cultured Despisers* (Cambridge: Cambridge University Press, 1988). Schleiermacher wrote the text to argue for the validity of the religious impulse in human life. He wrote it to the cultured elite of his day who he claimed regarded religion as vulgar, passé, and to be left behind for ethics, metaphysics, or other cultural activity. In Tillich's time, and even more so today, it is no doubt the case that the cultured despisers of religion are more likely to be atheists than those in Schleiermacher's time. Materialist metaphysics has become a kind of cultural default position with the rise of scientism, or the idea that what is really real about the universe is what we know

believe in God to look at their lives and see whether they have depth. Even if you reject religion, do you have a passion for art? Are you driven to pursue knowledge in some scientific field? Do you fight for social justice? Do you participate in loving forms of community? If your life has depth, and Tillich thought that at some level everyone's life does, then God is present in it. Tillich's analysis of the depths of life, not only as they are expressed in religion but in culture, and his claim that the presence of that depth is the presence of God is one of his most important ideas and one that can only be understood by clarifying the meaning of Tillich's understanding of God and God's relation to the universe.

Yet another reason for the relevance of Tillich's idea of God today is the compelling global need for interreligious understanding. Our world is not turning back from the globalizing trends that are dramatically reshaping it. The instantaneous, global communication systems we have set up mean that previously isolated cultures and individuals confront one another as never before. This confrontation often involves religious confrontation, and at times this confrontation has led to conflict. The historian can see that in the modern West, it took generations for Christian groups to learn to tolerate each other, and, at least for some, to move beyond toleration to a deepened understanding of one other. While the need for interreligious toleration and understanding is global, many of the representatives of religious traditions throughout the world do not have the advantage of having gone through the hard fought process that led in the West to an affirmation of religious freedom.

In this context of interreligious confrontation, Tillich's idea of God can play an important role. It has both a universal element and yet is able to account for vital individual differences among

---

through the natural sciences, and that knowledge is ultimately reducible to the reality of matter in motion.

religions. In this way, it avoids the pitfalls of either putting all religious traditions into isolated boxes that cannot understand one another or fusing them into a nondescript unity. It is also the case that Tillich's idea of God, like everything he analyzed, contains an inherent dynamic tension. Tillich never lost touch of the fact that religious passions indelibly contain an ultimate or absolute character and that this absoluteness is housed in the often fickle and very much finite form of human strivings. He also never lost sight of the constant danger religious traditions face insofar as they bear something ultimate in their idea of God but they do this in a finite form that is in constant danger of absolutizing itself. Tillich's analysis enables an understanding of the absolute passion of religion and the absolutization of religious ideals, even while it shows systematically the pitfalls and problems potentially involved with each. One of Tillich's genuine contributions is to show that because religion deals directly with ultimate matters like no other human endeavor, it is both absolutely necessary for its integrating and healing power, and it can go tragically and destructively wrong. This kind of analysis of religion and of Deity is important for understanding the tensions in our world today and to help point to a peaceful way forward that embraces rather than negates the significance of religious passion.[15]

[15] One of the themes of a movement in the early twenty-first century called "New Atheism" is that religious belief is responsible for much of the conflict in the world. New atheists envision a post-religious future as the solution to human conflict. They fail to give significant credence to the distinction between legitimate religious passion and illegitimate religious passion because they regard the source of human conflict as lying in religious passion as such. New atheists affirm an idea of deity that Tillich denies even while Tillich sees the movement of God in the depths of life as invariably involving religious passion. Religious passion is a key part of what makes us human. It can and sometimes does go wrong, but to lose it would mean to sink into a less than human condition. Important new atheist works include: Sam Harris, *The End of Faith: Religion, Terror, and the Future of Reason* (New

Finally, a book about Tillich's understanding of God is important because it abstracts a vital area of his thought that is difficult to access. In particular, what I develop in this book is what could be called Tillich's theory of God or the Divine. This theory belongs in the philosophy of religion rather than theology. In other words, my goal is not the explication of the particular Christian idea of God developed by Tillich. He explains that idea in a major section in the first volume of his *Systematic Theology*. Instead, I want what could be called his inter-religious theory of the Divine or the Sacred.

The reason I seek this theory, rather than the more focused Christian idea of God, is because of the broad role it can play in reflection on religion. It impacts philosophy and philosophers, as well as, potentially, the devotees of any and all religious traditions, and even those who deny the validity of any religious referent. Tillich's understanding of religious theory at this level is worthy of serious consideration and discussion.

The problem, as I mentioned above, is that Tillich wrote no single-volume work on God. Instead, his pinnacle achievement is his three volume *Systematic Theology*. He makes it clear in that work that he is a Christian theologian writing a constructive theology for the Christian church.[16] Famously, in the *Systematic Theology* he follows what he called the "method of correlation," which attempts to give the Christian answer to humans' existential questions.[17] Clearly, then, the *Systematic Theology* involves reflection on Christian doctrine. As Tillich explains in the work, theology

---

York and London: W.W. Norton, 2005); Richard Dawkins, *The God Delusion* (Boston and New York: Mariner Books, 2008); Christopher Hitchins, *God is not Great: How Religion Poisons Everything* (New York: Hatchette Book Group, 2007); and Daniel Dennett, *Breaking the Spell: Religion as a Natural Phenomenon* (New York: Viking Penguin, 2007).

[16] ST I 3-11.

[17] ST I 59-66.

itself is reflection on the symbols used in the living Christian community.

While the *Systematic Theology* contains Christian theology, it also contains much more than that. Certainly, it contains philosophy. In the method of correlation, on the "question" side, Tillich always makes a philosophical analysis of the human situation. This is a vital and distinctive feature of his thought.[18] But also in this

---

[18] The precise relationship between philosophy and religion within Tillich's thought is a much discussed topic in scholarship on Tillich. On one level, Tillich makes it clear that, as he understands it, philosophy is what is ordinarily called "metaphysics." As such, it is a reflective endeavor whose goal is to grasp the structure of being. This includes, for Tillich, a grasp of the distortions of this structure in existential life. In contrast, religion as religion is not reflective in the same way. It is an immediate response or a being grasped by the breakthrough of something ultimate or unconditioned. Yet, Tillich is also abundantly clear that this religious immediacy needs to be reflected upon. One must use philosophical tools and a reflective philosophical approach to do this. One needs the philosophy of religion to understand religion. And it is also the case that one must bring one's grasp of the structure of reality along with its distortions into relation with the religious immediacy. There must be a mode of thinking that is above the metaphysical analysis and its distortions, the religious immediacy, and the reflection on that immediacy. This mode of thinking needs to organize, systematize, and understand the whole. It is this mode of thinking that is present in Tillich's *Systematic Theology* and especially evident in his famous method of correlation.

For the sake of this text, I do not need to settle or extensively engage the issue of the relation between philosophy and religion other than to claim that in his thinking Tillich is deeply engaged with a philosophical grasp of reality, religious immediacy, and the philosophy of religion, the latter involving reflection on religious phenomena from a universal perspective. It is with Tillich's philosophy of religion that this text is primarily concerned. Two of the best book-length works that engage Tillich on the issue of the relation between philosophy and religion are by Robert Scharlemann, *Reflection and Doubt in the Thought of Paul Tillich* (New Haven and London: Yale University Press, 1969), and Langdon Gilkey, *Gilkey on Tillich* (Oregon: Wipf and Stock, 1990).

work, usually on the "answer" side of his method, he engages in religious theory, or the philosophy of religion. As Tillich develops the Christian answer to existential questions, he explains the Christian beliefs he expounds from the broader context of religious theory. For example, he does not just unfold the content of Christian revelation. He develops an understanding of Christian revelation from within the context of an inter-religious theory of revelation. He does not just elucidate the Christian idea of God. He develops an understanding of the Christian idea of God from an inter-religious theory of the Divine.

Tillich's religious theory of God is embedded within a system whose final outcome is a Christian theology. This theory must be abstracted from that context and compared and connected with what he says elsewhere when he discusses religious theory. It can be abstracted because, despite the claim that his systematic theology is done from the context of a particular Christian commitment, his religious theory makes a universal claim. It claims to understand religious phenomena in universal categories. This text is devoted to abstracting Tillich's religious theory of God.

The Structure of this Text

While this is not a work of Christian theology, it does emerge from a particular cultural context. As such, I approach the question of God from what I take to be the most common cultural presuppositions about God and God's relation to the universe. I call these presuppositions the generic monotheistic idea of God. For those who believe in God, those who reject belief in God, and those who do not know whether they believe in God or not, generic monotheism is deeply entrenched in the culture.[19] In ex

[19] According to the Pew Forum, 83% of Americans believe in God or a universal spirit and are either absolutely certain or fairly certain about that

plaining Tillich's understanding of God it is necessary to begin with some cultural touchstone about God, rather than from absolutely nowhere. This is where I begin.

The first two chapters of the text are intended to be read together. Chapter one deconstructs the monotheistic idea of God from a Tillichean perspective, while chapter two constructs Tillich's understanding of God. Chapter three examines, both historically and theoretically, two alternative understandings of God to Tillich's: Deism and Interventionist Theism. The fourth chapter engages questions of epistemology, or how one can know the truth of Tillich's understanding of God. The final chapters can be read independently, although together they form an important unit. Chapter five examines the God of religion, and chapter six the God of culture. For Tillich, the same ultimate meaning permeates both religion and culture, and the two must be understood in their unity and difference.

belief. *Religious Landscape Study,* http://www.pewforum.org/religious-landscape-study/belief-in-god/

Chapter 1

God: The Difficulties

One of the difficult things in writing a book about God is that there is a common cultural assumption about who or what God is that tends to call into question the need for such a book. Whether people believe in God or not, they regard God as a supernatural being who exists alongside or separate from the world. Assuming a monotheistic framework, God has certain agreed-upon attributes. God is eternal, meaning God has always existed and will always exist. God is all-powerful, meaning God can do anything. God is all-knowing, meaning God knows every piece of knowledge there is to know. God is completely good, so whatever God does is just and right.

Given this consensus about who God is, it is perhaps surprising to know that Paul Tillich, one of the most important Protestant theologians of modern times, disagreed with it so vehemently that he felt the need to attack it in order to attempt to break it down. Tillich's claim is that the common monotheistic idea of God as a being alongside the world with certain agreed upon attributes falsifies who or what God is. This falsification would, perhaps, be innocent or harmless enough, were it not for the fact that, according to Tillich, it so deeply fails to understand who God is and God's relation to us that it contributes to the lack of belief in God.[1]

In face of the common cultural monotheistic understanding of God, Tillich proposed an alternative. This book explains that alternative and its implications. Understanding Tillich's alternative is not an easy task. It is much easier to think of reality as being split into two distinct parts. In one part, there is the world and everything that exists within it. In the other part, there is God, an existing supernatural being with certain attributes. This is, however, precisely the understanding of God and the God-world relation that Tillich critiqued and that he argued needed replacement.

In this chapter, I develop Tillich's critique of the idea of God as an existing supernatural being with certain agreed upon attributes. Following Tillich, I want to problematize this idea of God in order to open the way for Tillich's alternative. In the following chapter, I explain Tillich's understanding of God and God's relationship to the universe before turning in the third chapter to an explanation of what is at stake in the different ideas of God being examined.

We begin the process of examining God and God's relationship to the universe with a general analysis of how we know things at all before moving to questions about the knowledge of God.

---

[1] A consistent theme in Tillich's thought was to trace the source of disbelief in God to an improper idea of God. This includes the idea of a God who is not needed because God is separated from the universe, while the universe and human culture are understood to be independent of God and running just fine on their own. It also includes the idea of God as a being in a realm alongside the world whose revelations require beliefs and corresponding actions that conflict with our emerging knowledge of the universe in the sciences and history, and our ethical understanding of ourselves. He summarizes these issues as the problems of what he calls "autonomy" and "heteronomy," or, at times, "secularization" and "demonization." They are covered extensively in chapter 3.

1. Human Knowing and the World

Sometimes when people say they want to *know* that God exists, they seem to mean they want to know that God is real like they know that a tree, a desk, or a book is real. These are things in the world that appear to us through our senses. But, of course, no one who believes in God thinks God is the kind of reality that can be known in this way: as an object given to our senses that appears in the world. Our knowledge of God has to be different from our knowledge of things in the world. In order to think about how we might know God, we begin by thinking about how we know things in the world. Modern philosophy has expended tremendous effort in attempting to explain how humans know things. Tillich was well versed in the philosophical traditions of modernity and articulated his own view in relation to them. We cannot review the history of the details and debates, but we can at least chart a course through this territory.

All knowing must somehow bring together the knower, or the subject, and what is known, or the object. What is true of reality outside of the mind must be given to the mind and adequately present in it in order for there to be genuine knowledge. As part of the modern debates about knowledge, philosophers developed sophisticated theories about what the mind itself contributes to the process of knowledge, what reality may be like apart from the grasp of it by our minds, and how we can possibly know either of these things.

The world of objects is given to the subject through the senses. Whatever we perceive through our senses is always temporally and individually given. We see this tree, this forest, this river, these mountains. While perception is individual, our mind grasps what is individually perceived by somehow applying universal concepts to it. Universal concepts apply to many individuals. We know this thing before us is a tree because of the universal idea of a tree that we apply to it. Because we can think in universals, we can categorize and understand our world. Again, there are many sophisticated philosophical theories about how this works, and there is an especially significant debate in the history of philosophy about whether things outside the mind are simply individual instances or whether they also have universal essences corresponding to the universal concepts by which we grasp them. For his part, Tillich thought things had universal essences, but universal essences were not static but subject to change and transformation over time.

All individual perception takes place and makes sense within some greater whole. Tillich called this whole the world. It is the structured unity in which every act of perception and knowledge occurs. In order to understand this whole, we need to account for more universal concepts than the concepts of things in the world. We need to account for things like time and space themselves, cause and effect, and substance and attributes.[2] These large formal categories apply to everything in the world. They structure the world. The universe as a whole, as well as human history that takes place within it, unfolds in time and space. Each moment of each

---

[2]The technical terminology is substance and accidents, but attributes better expresses the common meaning. We could go beyond these kinds of formal categories and ask whether we can articulate categories that grasp the fundamental structure of the world in all of its manifestations. This is the large question of what in philosophy is called metaphysics. Tillich himself was a metaphysician. He developed what he called a fundamental ontology for understanding the structure of the universe as it manifests itself in all realms of being. His mature ontology can be found in ST I 163-204. In a shorthand summary, Tillich thought in all of its manifestations, the universe expresses both a formal element, or an element of order and unity, along with a dynamic element, or an element that pushes against order and unity and is the source of transformation and change. He spent considerable time expressing how form and dynamics express themselves in the realms of pure matter, organic life, animal life, and human culture. All of these things are important for understanding Tillich's thought as a whole.

part of the universe, including human history, is the effect of which the previous moment is in some sense the cause.[3] Every individual object in the world is a substance with attributes.

2. Human Knowing and God

Objects in the world are known by being given to us through the senses. The subject is able to know these objects by means of concepts and the large formal categories that structure the world, like time, space, cause and effect, and substance and attributes. How does God fit into this? Commonly, the question of God involves the question of whether in addition to the world, there exists a supernatural being beyond the world who made it and rules over it. This is the common monotheistic idea of God with which we began. Put this way, to know God would mean for the subject to have a valid concept of a supernatural being with certain attributes that exists alongside the world.

As we have said, it is precisely this idea of God that Tillich critiques. We can reduce his critique to a general principle. Tillich claims that the concepts or categories of our minds that apply to the world cannot also be applied literally to God without limiting God and making God dependent on some aspect of the world.

To understand this critique, we need to grant a claim Tillich makes about our common idea of God. Tillich says that contained within the meaning of the word "God," at its deepest level, is the idea of that which is not dependent upon nor derived from any-

---

[3] Tillich affirmed human freedom but argued it could only be enacted from within a meaningful context that both made freedom possible but also limited it from ever being absolute. He equated the idea of absolute freedom, or the idea that one would absolutely create oneself from nowhere purely on the basis of one's own decisions, with arbitrariness.

thing in the finite world. The term he uses to express this is "aseity," which means "non-derived."[4] In the generic monotheistic idea of God, the world is understood as being dependent on God, but God is neither derived from nor dependent upon the world. If God was derived from or dependent on the world or anything outside of God, then something outside of God would determine God's being. It would be greater than God in the sense that God would be subject to it in order to be. God's aseity, then, is a protection or a boundary marker determining what cannot be said of God. God cannot be subject to anything in the world in order for God to be.

While we ordinarily may not think of it, Tillich claims that we apply categories taken from the world to God when we envision God as a supernatural being alongside the world with certain attributes. Minimally, we apply the categories of substance and attributes to God. We claim that God is an individual thing or substance, who is defined by certain characteristics or attributes like eternality, omnipotence, omniscience, and all-goodness. While this may seem innocent enough, substance and attributes are categories that define things that exist in the world. If we apply these categories to God, we subject God to categories that structure the world and make God dependent on those categories in order for God to be. In effect, we claim if there were not substance and attributes, there could be no God. God is dependent upon the structure of substance and attributes in order for God to be.

This highly abstract critique of Tillich's can be made clearer and more potent by showing the problematic character of literally applying the attributes of eternality, omnipotence, all-goodness, and omniscience to God. For Tillich, this attempt is rooted in a mistake. It is an understandable error, but an error nonetheless. The common monotheistic idea of God correctly affirms that God

---

[4] ST I 236, 248.

is greater than we are and greater than the world. The problem is, it attempts to express this by taking ideas of things from the world, extending them in a merely quantitative way, and then applying them to God. This subjects God to ideas taken from the world, violating the principle that God has aseity and is not dependent on anything in the world. We can show how this occurs with each of the four common attributes of God.

What do we mean when we say that God is eternal? In an unreflective moment, perhaps, we claim to mean that God was never born and God will never die. Perhaps better put, we claim that God has always existed and God always will exist. But what does that mean? Does it mean that God is in time like we are, only the time in which God exists extends infinitely into the past and infinitely into the future? Clearly, we live in time. We are aware that the fleeting present of our lives comes from a limited past and moves to a limited future. To understand that God is eternal, is it adequate merely to extend the arrow of time infinitely into the past and infinitely into the future and say that God lives from that infinite past into an infinite future?

Clearly, at this point, those who accept the common monotheistic idea of God balk at the notion that God's eternality means a quantitatively infinite extension of time. The reason this does not work is because it subjects God to time. Time is a category of the finite world but God is not finite, so God cannot be subject to this category. Whatever we mean by claiming that God is eternal, we do not mean that God lives infinitely subjected to time. God's eternality must mean that God is beyond time.

The same mistaken thinking can be shown in applying the attribute of omnipotence literally to God conceived as a being who exists alongside the world. Our finite minds have an idea of power taken from the world.[5] Even the strongest and most exalted of humans have limited power, however, and in order to acknowledge God's greatness, we do not want to affirm such limitations of God. It seems correct, therefore, to express God's greatness by quantitatively increasing the amount of power God has and claiming that God can do anything.

Increasing the amount of physical power quantitatively and applying it to God makes God into a sort of super-Superman. At this point, however, we invariably run into what seems intuitively to be silly questions. Since God can do anything, can God make a rock so heavy God cannot lift it? Can God make a wall so high God cannot scale it? The reason these kinds of questions seem silly or wrong is that they presuppose that God is a measurable power, only a really big one. God is still measured on the scale of power; God is just higher up on the scale than we are. These kinds of questions expose the fact that defining the all-powerfulness of God as God's ability to do anything places God on a quantitative scale of power, making God subject to that scale in order to be who or what God is.

One could claim that by calling God all-powerful, we mean that God has infinite power. This claim yields a contradiction, however, since physical power is a measurable quantity. One cannot actually possess an infinite amount of a measurable quantity because by definition it would be infinite and therefore immeasurable. In claiming that God is omnipotent we must mean something other than the idea that God has an infinite amount of the

---

[5] An important distinction can and should be drawn between physical power and social power. Physical power is the ability to accomplish some goal or realize some end through the use of measurable force. Social power involves having an impact on social relations. While both are ultimately important in thinking about God's power, it seems most generally to be the case that people have physical power in mind when thinking about the Divine omnipotence, so I limit my discussion here to physical power.

measurable quantity of power, in the same way that claiming God is eternal means something different than God is subject to an infinite quantity of time.

Applying the attributes of all-goodness and omniscience to God involves a unique way of thinking because goodness and knowledge are distinctly human realities in a way that time and power are not. Everything exists in time and everything has its own level or measure of power. However, only humans are capable of realizing and following a criteria of goodness in their relations with each other, and only humans are capable of knowledge. While animals are capable of some spontaneous activity in relation to their environments, ultimately, they follow what we often call instinct in their relation to the world and one another rather than a criteria of goodness. Likewise, animals are able to respond to their environments with awareness. They are keen to what is happening in their surroundings. Despite this, they lack full self-consciousness and the ability to grasp the world through universal concepts and the use of language. They cannot engage in the complex process of knowing that humans do. They cannot do science. Since applying goodness and knowledge to God involves applying distinctly human realities, we need to examine these realities.

The issue of goodness is admittedly complicated as there is a long and important debate in the history of Western thought, and human thought in general, about what determines a good act. Should we focus on the results of the act? Is there something about the act itself that tells us whether it is good or bad? What role do intentions play in determining the goodness of an act? How important is the goodness of one's character in determining the goodness of an act? These are all vitally important questions that we cannot solve here. We can point out, however, that the debate itself shows there is a criteria of goodness to be applied in our relationships with each other. Even if we do not agree precisely what that criteria is, the fact that we seek it and debate about it presupposes its presence.

And there are a lot of things in the ethical realm on which we can agree, whether we can articulate and agree on the precise reasons why we affirm them or not. We can agree it would be wrong to treat a person as if they were only a material object. We can agree that relationships should respect human freedom and not be abusive, although different cultures may draw the line for determining abuse differently. We can agree that things like stealing, killing, and lying are wrong, although we may disagree whether they are always wrong in all instances. Even within our disagreements, it remains the case that our lives are lived by a norm of goodness.

When we say that God is wholly good, and we mean by this that God always does what is right while we sometimes do what is right and sometimes what is wrong, we make the same mistake we make in literally applying the concepts of time and power to God: we make God greater than us in a merely quantitative way. God always does what is right while we do not always do so. But God is still subject to the norm of goodness just like we are. God must follow this norm to determine God's being, or who or what God is. Rather than God being independent and non-derived, God is subject to something outside of God's self that determines God's being.

The same mistake occurs when we apply knowledge to God. As stated earlier in the chapter, knowledge involves the unity of subject and object. Reflection on the attempt at this unity shows that the process of knowing is complicated. Certainly we are aware of our surroundings in an immediate sense and we can generally trust the world given to us through our senses good enough to get by in it. However, truly to know the world requires intense concentration and commitment, along with the correct methods being applied to the different types of objects that exist, as well as the back and forth of questioning and debate, in order to come to verifiable conclusions. The ongoing process of science in all fields proceeds in this way. The goal in all fields is to achieve unity between the objects being examined and the subject doing the examining. If we have such unity, we have knowledge or truth. The criteria of truth determines all knowing. It is the judgment about the unity between subject and object.

When we say that God knows everything and we mean this in a quantitatively extended sense, we subject God to the criteria of truth. Like us, God is a subject whose "mind" is united with the objects that God knows. While we only partially realize the criteria of truth, God fully realizes the criteria of truth for all possible objects for all time. This seems like a great claim to make of God, but God becomes subject to the criteria of truth which God must satisfy and act in accordance with in order to know things – just like us. In this way, the criteria of truth determines God in the same way that it determines us, it is just that God is better at meeting it than we are. If God is subject to the criteria of truth for God's knowledge, then God is dependent on something outside of God in order for God to be. God is not independent and non-derived, qualitatively different from everything in the universe that depends on God.

The problem we have been addressing in applying attributes to God is that when we quantitatively extend some aspect of finite reality and apply it to God in a high degree, we invariably make God subject to something finite in order for God to be. God may be a great power, but God remains just another power subject to the scale of power. God may have a great mind or a great will, but God's mind and will are subject to the same standards as our minds or wills in order to know things or do what is right. Tillich summarizes the conflict in this situation by saying there can be no "unconditional being...within reality." This idea is, he says, "a contradiction in terms."[6] What we always intend in our idea of God, to Tillich, is the idea of something unconditional. Whatever is unconditional is something to which the mind cannot apply its finite concepts and categories. It is something that cannot be put on any kind of scale or measurement taken from the finite world. When we think about God, we do not want a being that lives in an extended time, is a bigger power, or has a better mind and will. We want that which cannot be temporally measured or put on the scale by which we determine time, power, truth, and goodness. We want that which is the basis of the scale itself. That alone can express what we mean in the deepest sense when we refer to God. God has aseity and thereby God cannot be conditioned by anything outside of God's self. But how can we think about this kind of reality? How can we say anything about it? With these questions, we move to the heart of the difficulty in understanding Tillich's idea of God.

---

[6] ST I 207.

Chapter 2

God's Pervasive Presence

The intent of the previous chapter was to deconstruct the generic monotheistic idea of God as an existing supernatural being with certain attributes. The intent of this chapter is to construct Tillich's understanding of God and God's relationship to the world. In the process, I explain some of the most important symbols for God used by Tillich.

1. Infinity is not a thing but more than a thing

If God is not a supernatural being alongside the world, then who or what is God? The short answer to this, for Tillich, is that God is the infinite, ultimate, absolute, or unconditioned. To Tillich, on some level these highly abstract terms are unavoidable. They are terms that attempt to give credence to the reality of God, which is the reality of something that is not another thing, object, or substance in a supernatural world alongside this world. At one point Tillich says that referring to God with terms like infinite or unconditioned is to speak "rationally and ecstatically at the same time."[1] He means these terms refer to something, so they are rational. What they refer to, however, escapes being grasped by our concepts. Infinity, unconditionality, and absoluteness are not concepts of an object. They do not refer to some thing of which we have a corresponding concept, and, as such, can ever subsume or grasp with our minds. To use these terms, therefore, is to speak "ecstatically," or in a way that opens up to something that is real but ungraspable because it goes beyond our defining concepts.

If God is not a supernatural being alongside the world, then how does God relate to the world? For Tillich, the reality of God stands in a paradoxical relationship with the finite world. On the one hand, God is completely other than the finite world. There is a break, a gap, or a leap between God and the world such that no categories of anything in the world can apply to God. On the other hand, God is related to the world in the sense that God permeates and pervades it. God upholds the finite world and is infused through it. The infinite that is God, pervades the finite that is the world. But the infinite pervades the finite in such a way that it is never exhausted or completed in its permeating of the finite. It remains something that is inexhaustible and goes beyond, even while it is something that is here and present.

Tillich claims the understanding of God as that which is infinite but nevertheless present solves the classic problem of the relationship between the Divine immanence and Divine transcendence.[2] Christian theologians have long struggled with the question of how it is if God is a being "up there" or "out there," in other words, a transcendent supernatural being alongside the universe, then how can God also be "in here," or pervading the finite reality we experience? If God is "located" somewhere else, how can God be immanent? For Tillich, God is not located somewhere else.

---

[1] ST II 10.

[2] ST I 237.

God is the infinite depth within the finite, but as infinite that which is always inexhaustible and goes beyond the finite.

It is difficult to conceive of images that do justice to Tillich's idea of God. One could think geometrically of multiple lines that come from infinity to intersect a sphere at a single point and extend infinitely beyond that point in all directions. The sphere where they intersect is the finite world. What is present in the intersection is something infinite and ungraspable that goes endlessly beyond the point of intersection. Or, one could think of a translucent sphere with dozens of small holes in it and a bright light inside. The light shines through the sphere, pouring out of all the holes into the infinity of space. However inadequately, these images at least point to Tillich's idea of God as the infinite that is within the finite, but in it as something that is ungraspable and goes infinitely beyond the finite at the same time.

Another technical term Tillich uses to refer to God is "being-itself." He says directly, "The being of God is being-itself."[3] Being-itself is a philosophical category. It is part of metaphysics and metaphysics is that part of philosophy that seeks to grasp the primordial structure and character of reality. If we say that something is, or something has being, what do we mean in the deepest, and yet most complete, richest, and fullest sense? That is a philosophical question and those of us in the West can look to the inheritance of Greek thought, as well as the history of Jewish, Christian, and Muslim thought for responses to it. With this category, Tillich connects the religious understanding of God with the history of philosophical reflection.

To explain being-itself requires explaining Tillich's use of the term "being." Following a deep philosophical tradition in the West, for Tillich, "being" is not an empty category that refers to everything that exists. We often use the term that way. We think

[3] ST I 235.

of "being" like a big box, and everything that exists is within this box. This use of the term treats it as the most formal and empty category there is. Tillich's understanding of the term is exactly the opposite of the most formal and empty category. To Tillich, "being" is absolute richness and absolute fullness.

As absolute richness and fullness, for Tillich, whatever is great about life, whatever is expressive, joyful, creative, and connecting is full of being. For Tillich, when we examine the different realms of being that exist, from mere matter in motion to plants, animals, and finally humans, we move from things that are less full of being to those that are more full of being.[4] Greater elements of reality are incorporated into plants and animals than mere matter in motion. Animals are an indissoluble unity of parts and are capable of some spontaneous action in relation to their environ-

---

[4] With this claim, we touch a complex part of Tillich's metaphysics. On the one hand, Tillich makes it clear that it is in the human realm where the fullest expression of being is realized. He calls the human being, "microcosmos," and claims that it is in human reality where we see and experience the depth of the universe or the depth of being (See ST I 168-186, especially 176). On the other hand, Tillich is a subtle metaphysician. For him, while the deepest expression of being is realized in the human realm, it is also the case that the basic elements of being are present in all realms of being. In other words, his metaphysics opens to both the difference and the unity between the human realm and other realms. So, for example, to Tillich, humans alone experience the fullness of freedom because humans alone can separate themselves from their immediate environment in such a way that they can deliberate about options regarding an action to take, and make a decision for which they bear responsibility. However, in animals something like freedom must be present, though in a lesser, rudimentary form. Animals are not just automatons whose every act can be calculated with mathematical precision. They too have a center that acts with spontaneity and even creativity. Tillich would embrace studies on animal emotions and animal intelligence, affirming the reality of each, even while he would never want us to forget that what is realized in animals is not identical with what is realized in the human.

ment. In this, they incorporate certain elements of reality, like being individuals and acting spontaneously, in ways that plants and mere matter in motion do not incorporate. This is not to denigrate either mere matter in motion or plants. Everything that exists expresses being in its own way, and, to Tillich, this is what makes it great.[5] Tillich also stresses that all realms of being are interrelated and interdependent. There can be no animals without matter in motion and plants, just as there can be no humans without all of the other groups.[6] Still, it remains the case that the movement from plants to animals involves a greater and deeper realization of being, even as the movement from animals to humans involves the same.

The realm of animals differs from the realm of humans because the latter is the realm of full self-consciousness, complete individuality, the use of universal concepts and language to grasp reality, and the ability to shape one's life through free decisions. With these latter kinds of attributes, human beings have the most "being" of any creature. For Tillich, when you reach the realm of human beings, you break through to what he often calls the realm of meaning.[7] Because we are fully self-conscious and free creatures, we are able to create a realm of meaning in which we live through our decisions. We do not just follow laws, like matter in motion, or instinct, like animals. We create a realm of culture where we both take in reality and insert ourselves into it in distinct ways. We realize meaning in science, technology, art, religion, and in our relationships with each other where we work for just and

---

[5] ST III 88-92.

[6] Tillich calls this the "multi-dimensional unity of life." He analyzes the different dimensions of life in terms of their evolutionary emergence from matter to plants, animals, and humans (ST III 11-30).

[7] This is especially clear in Tillich's early German works from the 1920's. See SS 149-152, and PR 56-72.

loving forms of community. All of this is the highest expression of being of which we are aware.

When Tillich says God is being-itself, he is claiming that whatever richness, expressivity and fullness there is in life, or whatever "being" it has, it emerges from the basis of an infinite fullness that is in it, or "being-itself." Being-itself cannot be thought of as another being, or a kind of thing that occupies the highest rung on the ladder of beings. In other words, it is not the case that there is matter in motion, plants, animals, humans, and then God or being-itself, at the top of the ladder as the highest kind of being. If this were the case, we would have to ask what it is that gives the things in every realm of being their fullness, richness, and power. We would have to ask this of every level, including the level upon which we put God. Whatever it is that gives to everything on every level of being its richness, fullness, and power would be something greater than God because it would be that which gives God fullness, richness, and power in whatever degree God has them. God would depend on whatever gives God these things in order to be. God would simply be one of the manifestations of whatever is beyond God. This is why Tillich makes such an effort to say that God is not "a being." God does not occupy a rung on the ladder of beings, even the top rung. God is the source of the richness, fullness, and power within everything. God is being, or the inexhaustible fullness of being in and beyond all beings. God is being-itself.

Being-itself not only refers to richness and fullness of being but also to power in specified ways for Tillich. Power often has a negative connotation. We think of it as forcefulness or the kind of power someone might have over someone else that is oppressive or manipulative. Tillich certainly understands this and he has ways to account for it in his thought, but almost all of the time when he refers to power, it is a positive category. For Tillich, power means becoming what you were meant to be or realizing your potential in a life process. It means actualization. When an acorn sprouts and becomes an oak tree, it is realizing or expressing its power. It will do this through its entire life as it cycles nutrients through itself and grows. Humans express power in their locomotion like all animals, but we also express it in developing our minds and unique talents and realizing our creative potential. We express power by engaging in social groups to pursue projects of all kinds, large and small. As being-itself, God is not only absolute fullness and richness but the capacity to realize endless potentialities and creativity, a capacity that lies within the depths of reality.

While being-itself as power is the source of creative potentialities, it is also, in its root, the sheer power-to-be. Tillich says we can get at least some sense of this sheer power of being if we imagine everything vanishing – the entire universe and all of its beings and features. We can think this way because we can think beyond everything finite, including the finitude of our individual lives and the history of the universe as a whole. We can look at the world around us and imagine it not being there. When we do this, we imagine pure "non-being." Everything is swallowed by non-being.

Tillich describes this state of imagining as a "metaphysical shock" and he claims that the beginning of reflection about being must be rooted in something like this shock.[8] This metaphysical shock does not refer to an actual condition and it can never be an actual condition for the thinking subject because to imagine everything sinking into non-being requires a subject doing the imagining and thereby avoiding non-being! As Tillich says, "Thought must start with being...."[9] It begins with what-is and is grounded on it, not with what is not. However, while this metaphysical

[8] ST 1 163.

[9] ST 1 163.

shock is not an actual condition, it is a telling one. It imaginatively takes one beyond all of the things and features that are present in experienced reality, including the reality of one's own self. Beyond features, beyond the discriminations of types of being, in imagining that everything sinks into the abyss of non-being, one experiences in a raw or more pure way the fact that "being-is." Things stand out of non-being. In transcending all features of being by imagining them sinking into non-being, we encounter the pure power of being.

This metaphysical shock at least gives us some sense of the root power of being-itself. It is the power-to-be that stands against utter nothingness, or what Tillich calls "absolute non-being." For Tillich, everything in every realm of being, all matter in motion, plants, animals, and human beings, have their own finite power of being. Each thing is capable of realizing its potentialities in a finite and limited way. But the universe as a whole and every realm of being together has its limited power of being only because it shares in the absolute power of being that is being-itself. It is being-itself that is the source of all life, all potentialities, and all creativity because it is the pure power to be vis-à-vis absolute nothingness.

As stated in the first chapter, one of the most important ideas for understanding God, to Tillich, is the idea of "aseity." The term literally means "non-derived," or "non-dependent." As being-itself, God has aseity. God has within Godself the power to stand out of pure non-being and give to everything that exists its power to be. God is the absolute source of whatever fullness, richness, and creative potentialities there are in reality, but as the source of all fullness, richness, and creative potentialities, God is not subject to them or measured by them as another being.

As the absolute power-to-be, God is not another measurable power alongside the powers of the finite world. God is the absolute power that is within and that makes possible all finite power.

This is the root meaning of God's omnipotence. Likewise, God is not an existing being alongside the world that is completely good or that knows all possible information there is to know. Instead, God is the absolute source of all goodness and knowing that is within and that makes possible each act of goodness and knowing. This is the root meaning of the Divine goodness and Divine omniscience. It is only if we think of God's omnipotence, goodness, and omniscience as the infinite basis of power, goodness, and knowing, that we can preserve God's aseity. This means that the God who has aseity is not an existing being alongside the world, but being-itself.

This brief introduction to what Tillich means by God is admittedly abstract. I develop it further by explaining some of the most common terms or phrases Tillich uses to refer to God. Before proceeding to that, however, I need to explain Tillich's understanding of symbolic language for God.

2. Religious Symbols for God and the God-World Relationship

The argument of chapter one was that no categories taken from the finite world can literally apply to God because they subject God to the world. This would have to be true of categories that express God's relationship with the world as well. The categories of our finite minds that express relationality, like cause and effect, and substance and attributes, apply to relationships between things in the finite world. If we apply the categories that express the relationship between things in the finite world to God's relation to the world, we subject God to the categories of relations within the finite world. And yet, if we cannot apply relational categories from the world to understand the God-world relation, how can we understand or express that relation at all?

This latter question is an especially important one for Tillich's thought because Tillich claims that God, or the infinite, impresses Godself upon the finite world, including the world of human meanings, at all times. If God's reality is there, somehow making its presence felt and known, and somehow making a difference in human life, then we have to be able to talk about it and have some way of understanding how God's presence is felt and known.

The issue of how we can have meaningful language for God and God's relation to the world is a deeply complex problem in all reflection about God. It is the problem of how we can know God, who is unknown. Tillich's resolution to this problem is to claim that all language about God and God's relationship to the world must be symbolic and not literal. He develops a theory of symbols to explain what he means.

For Tillich, a symbol is something that points beyond itself to something else. Its message or the reality it is trying to convey is beyond it. In this way, symbols can be compared to signs. We use signs all the time. The letters on this page are signs that point to something else. They point to words, sentences, and ideas about reality I am trying to express. A red light at an intersection is a sign. It points beyond itself, telling motorists to stop. The difference between symbols and signs is that signs are arbitrary markers pointing to some reality. Potentially, they can be replaced at will. We could all decide that an orange light should mean stop and a blue light should mean go. Practically, this would be difficult to implement, but on a theoretical level we can understand it as being possible. While signs are arbitrary markers, this is not the case with symbols. There is a deeper relationship between the symbol and what it represents than there is with signs. In Tillich's language, a symbol "participates in that to which it points."[10] He

[10] DF 42.

means that a symbol makes something beyond itself be present, but it does so by sharing in the life of that reality.

Tillich uses the example of a national flag as a symbol.[11] The flag points beyond itself to the nation it represents. Its colors and the features on it say something about that nation. We could say that in a flag, a nation is present. It is, of course, not the case that every detail about the nation is there or every life of every citizen is inscribed there. However, something about what the nation stands for is represented by the flag and whatever this is has been embraced by a group of people who claim this flag as representing their nation. If a nation is destroyed by another power, or if a nation goes through a significant upheaval so that its identity is transformed in a major way, the old flag is no longer adequate to represent it. A new flag must be developed.

A sports team's logo is another example of a symbol. The logo says something about the team and the place from where it comes. Fans wear clothing with the logo on it or they put stickers on their vehicle or decorate their rooms with the logo, because seeing the logo makes the team present. The logo participates in the reality of the team. Again, what is present with the logo is not every detail of the team. Not every player on every roster in the history of the team is literally to be accounted for with the logo. But some sort of distilled essence of the team is present in the logo.

We use symbols all of the time. They make our lives vivid and rich. Tillich makes the point that symbols open up deep aspects of reality to us, aspects of which we would not otherwise be aware.[12] Music, the visual arts, and literature especially have the power to open the depths of reality to us. However, there has to be a difference between symbols that point beyond themselves and

---

[11] DF 42.

[12] DF 42-43.

refer to other things within the world, and symbols that point to God. God is not another reality in our world that could be grasped and explained by a concept or known in another way. God can *only* be known through symbols.

Following a deep theological tradition, Tillich claims that God and the relationship between God and the world can be grasped through symbols because of what is called the "analogy of being."[13] God is being-itself, or the absolute source of everything that has being. Being-itself cannot literally be described with concepts taken from the world, but as the source of all things in the world, there must be an analogy or a likeness between the absolute source (God) and the world.

The analogy of being opens the possibility of meaningful symbols for God. The symbols, however, do not describe God literally. Symbolic language for God makes the reality that is beyond all concepts present only in an indirect and non-literal way. This means that in the use of symbols it is always the case that while something meaningful is said, whatever is said must also be negated. Explaining symbols of God always involves "it must be like this and yet not like this." Needless to say, this makes language about God tremendously complicated.

According to Tillich, it is the task of theology to explain the symbols of God used in a religious tradition, whatever that tradition is. In other words, theology is a secondary reflective endeavor that operates within a living religious tradition. What comes prior to theology is always the immediate religious experience of being-itself expressed in symbols. The theologian works behind that experience with the task of explaining what the symbols mean. This is what Tillich claims to be doing in his mature and culminating work, the *Systematic Theology,* vol's I, II, III. He is not describing who or what the object God is. He is explaining the distinctive

[13] ST I 239-240.

Christian symbols for God, or the way being-itself is present in Christian experience through a particular set of symbols for God. Tillich would expect theologians in other religious traditions to do the same in their theologies.[14]

While Tillich stresses it is the job of the theologian to explain the symbols of a particular living tradition in his *Systematic Theology*, he also does more than this in that work. He does things like explain why we must use symbols for God in the first place and how symbols for God operate. This is part of what is called the philosophy of religion. The claims he makes at this level of analysis are relevant for all religious expressions, not just the Christian theology that Tillich himself eventually does.

In Tillich's thought, part of the philosophy of religion involves the critique of the idea of God as a supernatural being and makes clear the symbolic nature of all approaches to Deity. Tillich knows that most people, and even, perhaps, most theologians commonly think of God as a discrete supernatural being with attributes. Monotheists, polytheists, and atheists all picture God or the Gods as a powerful being or beings. In monotheism, the deity is most commonly imaged as male and identified as a leader or someone with social authority. God is King, Lord, and Father.

---

[14] What is distinctive about Tillich's work, particularly in the *Systematic Theology*, is that he does not just dive in and begin explaining symbols for God. What he does first is analyze the realm of reality to which a symbol most basically relates. Does a certain symbol for God most basically relate to the broken and fragmented character of our existence (Tillich thinks the symbol of Christ does this)? Does a symbol for God most basically relate to our experience as historical beings whose individual histories are part of the larger history of humanity (Tillich thinks the symbol of the Kingdom of God does this)? Tillich locates and explains the meaning of Christian symbols insofar as they refer to relatively distinct realms of life. The execution of this procedure is what he calls, famously, his "method of correlation" and, in an important sense, this method organizes the structure of his mature theological work.

Clearly, thinking of God in this way is and has been an effective symbol in human history. In corporate worship as well as personal prayer and devotion, believers encounter the reality of God through the image of a powerful and yet caring supernatural being. This image or symbol makes God present.

While this symbol of God is extraordinarily effective, Tillich is adamant that we cannot lose sight of its symbolic character. For Tillich, what is meant in imaging God as a supernatural being is being-itself. This is what the symbol participates in and points to. At times, Tillich expresses this in quite creative language. He says, for example, "God is unconditioned, that makes him God; but the 'unconditional' is not God."[15] Or, "God is symbol for God."[16] What he means by these statements is that the referent of all images of God is the ultimate, the unconditioned, or being-itself. Religious activity, which involves everything from corporate worship to private prayer, is the realm of concrete images, of symbols. It is through these symbols that being-itself, the ultimate, or the unconditioned, is manifest. Philosophy of religion explains how this is the case. A particular theology interprets what the symbol means to those who experience it as a living symbol.

3. Tillich's Preferred Symbols for God

The philosophy of religion clarifies that all language for God is symbolic and refers to being-itself, not a supernatural being. In keeping with this important idea, Tillich develops within his work a distinctive set of symbols for God that are more generic than the symbols of a particular tradition but also less abstract than the terms for God used earlier like "infinite," "ultimate," "absolute," or

---

[15] TC 24.

[16] DF 46.

"being-itself." Tillich appears to have chosen these symbols because while they are concrete, they help avoid the mistaken notion that God is a supernatural object alongside the world. One could call them the common symbols of Tillich's philosophy of religion. These symbols include "ground of being," "power of being," and "depth of being." When referring to human culture in particular, Tillich often calls God the "ground of meaning," or "depth of meaning."[17] Since these symbols occur again and again in Tillich's writings, I explain them and what they mean in Tillich's thought.

---

[17] The categories of substance and accidents, and cause and effect are important categories for expressing the relationship between things within the world. Tillich stresses that neither can function literally to express the relationship between God and the world although both can interpret that relationship symbolically. If God is the substance of the world, then God manifests God's self in the features of the world, which are God's accidents. There must be some truth to this understanding of the God-world relation, since the infinite expresses itself in the finite. If this is taken literally, however, God becomes limited to the world and the world becomes limited to God, since a substance is fully expressed in its accidents. This is, in effect, the position of pantheism, which denies the transcendence of God to the world and the freedom of the world in relation to God. Alternatively, one could claim that God is the cause of the world and the world is the effect of God's causality. Again, there must be something true about this expression of the relationship between God and the world since God has aseity and is being-itself while the world relies on God for its being. However, as Tillich points out, cause and effect always form a series. What is effect at one point is cause at the next point. All of the conditions of the current moment in time are the effect of the previous moment in time, and they are the cause of the next moment in time. Cause and effect form an endless series both backward and projected forward in time. If God's relationship with the world is expressed as cause and effect, God is brought into or made subject to this series. God would essentially be the effect of a previous cause. If one makes the claim that God is an uncaused cause that underlies the series of cause and effect, in Tillich's understanding, this is claiming the category of causality cannot be applied literally to God. Instead, causality is being applied as a symbol. And, at this point, as Tillich says, causality essentially coincides with

The choice of the term "ground" in "ground of being" reverses the traditional biblical spatial imagery for God, since in the latter, God is considered up in heaven. Even though he does not explain it, Tillich appears to prefer the symbol of ground because it expresses support, while also expressing both nearness and indefiniteness. The ground is what upholds all things – or at least all things on earth. It is always near. We rely on it without thinking about it. At the same time, as a term, it is indefinite and unspecified. Ground includes soil, substrate, cement, and even fields, hills, and mountains. It includes everything upon which everything else stands. It is ubiquitous, and yet, expressed as merely "ground," it is unspecified, and so it serves as an effective symbol for being-itself as that in which everything is rooted, and yet is beyond all specifications.

The limits of the symbol ground of being for expressing God's relation to the world appear in the lack of interpenetration between the ground and what is grounded by it. Perhaps with plants, and especially trees with their deep roots, we can have a deeper image of the interpenetration of the ground and what is grounded by it, but generally it is easy to lose sight of the interrelation since the ground and what is on the ground are spatially separate. God's relationship to the world expressed as "power of being" and "depth of being" each in their own way express this interpenetration between God and the things of the world.

---

the category of substance as a symbol. To say that God is the cause underlying the causal series is identical to saying God is the substance underlying all that occurs. (*ST* I 238) In fact, Tillich almost never uses the categories of substance and accidents, or cause and effect to refer to God's relationship to the world. Presumably this is because of the danger of literalizing and misunderstanding them as expressions of the God-world relation. Much more commonly, Tillich uses the symbolic terms "ground of being," "power of being," and "depth of being."

As the power of being that makes all things be, God's relationship with all things is immanently interpenetrating. Analogies to this interpenetrating relation would include the power of gravity, which, though unseen, interpenetrates and thereby effects all things, or the power of one's own locomotion that is an interpenetrating aspect of one's whole being but is not located in one particular compartment of one's being.

God's relationship to the world expressed as "depth of being" expresses interpenetration as well, while also opening in a special way to what is traditionally called the divine transcendence. Again, reversing the traditional image for God as in the heavens, Tillich claims that God is in the depths.[18] The depths express something unfathomable and beyond, yet still connected with an appearing surface. Relating the image of depth to water, the depth of a lake is connected to the surface of the lake because of the formlessness and ubiquity of water. We can also think of the depths of the self, as the indelible aspects of one's personality, or those things which most deeply and meaningfully connect with and express one's way of being in the world. These depths are not separate from the appearing self, but are connected to it even while they go beyond what merely appears. Analogously, God as the depth of being expresses what is most indelible about reality while still being connected with all of the forms of reality experienced in the world.

Sometimes in speaking of God's relation to human culture, Tillich refers to God as either the "ground of meaning," the "ground of being and meaning," or the "depth of meaning." As we said above, it is only in human culture and human experience that

---

[18] Tillich also uses abyss to refer to the divine transcendence. He sometimes pairs it with ground and calls God the "ground and abyss of being." In this construction, ground refers to the imminent, upholding aspect of God and abyss the transcendent unknowable depths (See explanation at ST I 155-157).

the distinctive realm of meaning appears. Only humans stand apart from their condition enough that they can act freely and be creative in relationship to that condition. In human culture alone, do questions of normative meaning arise. Tillich claims that at their highest level these questions arise in the process of religious experience, scientific knowing, aesthetic expression, and moral reasoning about just and loving relationships and communities. For Tillich, whenever meaning appears, the depth of meaning appears with it. The infinite penetrates the entirety of the finite and appears in and through every part. In human culture, awareness of this depth appears in a special and powerful way as the depth of meaning.

Chapter 3

Alternatives for the God-World Relationship

Why does it matter whether God is conceived as a being alongside the world with certain attributes, or being-itself? What is at stake in the translation to thinking about God as being-itself?

Tillich knows that throughout most of history, most people thought of God or the Gods as beings. At one point, he calls this the position of "natural literalism."[1] There is something natural about projecting God or the Gods as beings more powerful than us residing in heaven above or alongside the world. However, to Tillich, we live at a time and in a place where a kind of critical consciousness has emerged that makes this position no longer viable. This is not just because we know there is no edge to space above or beyond us where God resides. It is also owing to a series of intellectual developments that have occurred over the past several hundred years that Tillich thinks must be taken seriously. No one chooses the time or the place in which they are born. However, everyone inherits religious, cultural, and intellectual trends because of the time and place in which they are born.

---

[1] DF 52-53.

Tillich is famous for giving what can be called "meta-analyses" of history. He often categorizes entire historical periods as being focused around a particular question or concern, or as being shaped by particular intellectual features or dynamics. The danger of this kind of analysis is that it invariably overlooks particulars. At the same time, if this kind of analysis is not made, the examination of history and its dynamics is reduced to particulars that do not add up to anything.

In analyzing the modern era in the West, Tillich regards it as a time where what he calls "autonomy" emerged. Autonomy means "self-law," but, as Tillich explains, it is best understood as the law of reason. During what is called the period of the Enlightenment, roughly the mid-seventeenth through the mid-nineteenth centuries, a new pattern of thinking emerged in Western Europe and the American Colonies/States. It essentially said, trust your reason. The human mind can know what is true about reality and the difference between right and wrong on its own. We do not have to turn to traditional authorities, whether those authorities are the authorities of the state (the Monarch) or the church (church leaders/the Bible), to know what is true and what is good. We can discover the true and the good, and follow their leading by ourselves.

Along with philosophical reflection, the emergence of autonomy involved the flourishing of all the sciences. This included all scientific fields, from the natural sciences with its newly discovered empirical method, to the social sciences and history. Rigorous methods of knowing were and still are being developed and refined in all areas with the common presupposition that there need be no submission to a traditional authority, religious or otherwise, in order to discover truth. In fact, not only does one not need to submit to an authority to discover truth, religious and secular authorities were and are open to being critiqued by the truths discovered by reason. Rather than simply submit to the Bible to tell us what is true about science or history, which was the pattern followed in the Middle Ages and the era of the Protestant Reformation, the Enlightenment changed all of this. The Bible could and can now be judged by the scientist or the historian.

Much of Enlightenment thinking looks simplistic to us today. Looking back, many Enlightenment thinkers seemed naïve about the power of reason to discover everything in a way everyone can agree on. Still, Tillich's insight into this period is a significant one, as modernity is the time in which autonomous thinking emerged and the period we can point to for unleashing a new way of being that affirms the power to know and to guide oneself by reason while also being free to criticize traditional authorities like the Bible and church teaching. We in the modern Western world have inherited this way of thinking and being, which is evident not just in the sciences but in our cultural life. Art, music, literature, and film are independent forces in the culture and are not subject to religious control or oversight. Deep meanings about life emerge through these creative forms of expression, but those meanings need not and often do not align themselves with Christian teaching. Arguments for how we should arrange society so that, for example, we have a just distribution of wealth, make sure people are treated fairly in their labor and their personal lives, and assure that those who need help are in fact given assistance, are often made independent of religious commitments. The autonomous pursuit of knowledge, art, and just and loving forms of community are all vital aspects of our cultural life.

This does not mean that religion has lost its significance. Certainly it too is still a vital and viable force in our culture and in many people's lives. It is also important as a background element that shapes the scientist's knowing, the artist's creating, and the social critic's vision for a just world. But while religion is still important, its importance must be understood from within the context of vital autonomous forces, many of which decry and reject religion in explicit ways. This was the world Tillich knew in his time, and, broadly speaking, it remains the world of our own time. While religion holds sway in many people's lives, we must account for and seek to understand powerful and important forces of autonomy within the culture.

Tillich's understanding of God needs to be placed within the context of the emergence of autonomy described here. This is the fundamental background from which his theology was done.[2] In this chapter, we examine the implications or meaning of his understanding of God by presenting his idea of the God-world relationship alongside two other ways of understanding that relationship. We look at the emergence of autonomy and the implications of autonomous thinking for each of the ways of understanding the God-world relationship.

1. Deism

Deism was a belief system largely embraced by aristocratic figures during the Enlightenment period of the mid-seventeenth through the mid-nineteenth centuries. It was never a movement with great mass appeal. There never was a full-blown Deist church or Deist revivals.[3] In fact, some people who held Deist positions, like Thomas Jefferson, felt the need to keep their views under wraps because their beliefs involved a critique of traditional Christian

---

[2] In the final lecture of his life Tillich summarized the purpose of his *Systematic Theology* as "the discussion or the answering of questions coming from the scientific and philosophical criticism of Christianity;" in other words, from the emergence of autonomy. "The Significance of the History of Religions for the Systematic Theologian," in FR 91.

[3] Many early Unitarians had much in common with Deism. In that sense, Deism, at least of a certain type, was connected with an organized religious tradition.

doctrine. Despite these things, it was an important enough position to develop a common literature and broadly agreed upon set of ideas.

Those who affirmed Deism sought a rational religion, as Deism emerged and overlapped with the Enlightenment or the Age of Reason in the West. Enlightenment thinkers thought human beings were finally transcending past eras of human history in which the human mind was sunk in superstition. People believed in fantastical things because we failed to use our minds or our reason. We turned to authorities, especially religious authorities like the Bible or church leaders, to tell us what is good and what is true instead of doing what we should be doing, which is using our reason and discovering what is good and what is true on our own. Deists sought a religion that accorded with what they regarded as the human goal, which was to live a life in accord with reason.

For Deists, the universe was rational and orderly. The emerging sciences were showing this. Such a universe must have been made by a rational and orderly God. The pursuit of science was regarded as thinking God's thoughts after him and grasping the rationality God put into creation.

If God had an exalted and rational mind, then God did not make mistakes when God made creation. God made human beings with adequate minds to discover the truth on their own. This included discovering who God is. Humans did not need special revelation from God in history to know about God or the universe. God made human beings with adequate wills so they could do what is good. God did not have to intervene to correct the wayward wills of humanity or fix what was helplessly broken in human beings. In general, Deists were optimistic about human capacities to do what is good, and they believed God gave humans immortal souls that guaranteed eternal happiness corresponding to good actions.

Sometimes Deist beliefs are summarized as believing in God, freedom, and immortality. God is creator, but God does not intervene in the world God has created. The world runs on its own like a top that continues to spin after one pulls the string or a car that continues to run after having been started. Humans are free and responsible. We are made upright, with the capacity to choose the good and to do it. Humans are immortal and will live eternally.

Deists thought their set of ideas expressed what all religion was truly about. They emerged from a Christian context. As such, they thought that at its core, the things they affirmed were what Christianity was truly about. They thought if someone removed the husk or shell from Christianity and got to its kernel, one would find Deist beliefs. This is why a Deist like Thomas Jefferson, although he veered from Christian beliefs, did not simply turn his back on Christianity and walk away from it. As a good Deist, Jefferson did not believe in the biblical miracles. At his home at Monticello, he used scissors to cut out all of the purported miracles from the New Testament gospels. What was left when the miracles were cut out, according to Jefferson, was Jesus' moral teaching. It was, according to him, "the most sublime and benevolent code of morals which has ever been offered to man."[4] This is what Christianity was about in essence to a Deist like Jefferson.

It is not surprising that a Deist church never emerged since the God of Deism is a distant God and not the kind of God with whom one interacts. There is no need in Deism for an immediate connection with God. God and the world are separate. The world is a rational and orderly mechanism. When we use our reason to

[4] Endrina Tay, "The Life and Morals of Jesus of Nazareth," 10/1/2014https://www.monticello.org/site/research-and-collections/life-and-morals-jesus-nazareth. An accessible summary of Deist thought by a contemporary of Jefferson is Thomas Paine, *The Age of Reason* (CreateSpace Independent Publishing Platform, 2015).

understand the world, we imitate God. In understanding the universe, we marvel at its creator. When we act morally, we live according to God's plan for us. But we are not connected to God in our daily lives.

For Tillich, the position of Deism represents an extreme form of autonomy. Humans are completely on their own to live lives of reason. God is distant. For Tillich, separating God from the world and turning the world into a mechanism cuts off access to the depths of reality. From a Tillichean perspective, we could describe this position as one in which reality is flat. As we have said, for Tillich, the term "being" is a term of depth that refers to the fullness, richness, and expressivity within all things ultimately rooted in being-itself. For the Deist position, "being" is a formal and empty category that refers to everything that is. Everything moves in an orderly and mechanistic way, as should human beings in knowing the world and following their ethical reasoning.

Cutting itself off from God, this position lacks depth, to Tillich. Its optimism is also problematic. Enlightenment Deists thought things could be known in universal, provable ways so that everyone with a rational mind could agree on them. Humans could know the right thing to do and when they knew it, they would do it. Progress was inevitable. This kind of optimism belies the need for any kind of healing, integrating, or sustaining powers that religion might provide. This position accounts neither for the depths of abundance and fullness in life, nor the depths of anxiety, alienation, and brokenness that are so much a part of life.

At the center of Tillich's life were two major world wars. He was 28 years old when WWI began. He volunteered and served as a chaplain, where he witnessed some of the worse carnage of the war. He saw the hopeful time of the post-war Weimar Republic in Germany give way to Nazism. Because he was a Socialist and because he resisted the Nazis, he was forced into exile from his native Germany in 1933. He was 53 years old when WWII began, and, when it ended, he described the time after the war as a void. In a striking comment from 1951, he says "It is not an exaggeration to say that today man experiences his present situation in terms of disruption, conflict, self-destruction, meaninglessness, and despair in all realms of life."[5] The tragic circumstances of his life and his time forced him to account for the fractured and estranged character of life and belied any belief in easy optimism or inevitable progress.

For Tillich, an autonomous situation reflected in a worldview like Deism loses vital touch with the sources of integration and healing that are needed at all times, but especially in times of chaos and destruction. Those sources are most explicitly religious sources. The ground of being is what holds things together when they begin to spin apart. Being-itself overcomes non-being, and a life consciously and experientially rooted in being-itself is able to overcome the threat of anxiety and disruption to it. I cover the healing power of religion in greater depth in chapter five. As stated above, for Tillich, autonomy is a valuable insight. It is valuable for humans to stand on their own and be able to seek knowledge and modes of living without simply turning to authorities to know what to believe and how to act. However, an autonomous situation that cuts itself off from the ground of being and meaning is a shallow situation and lacks the power to overcome disruptive and destructive threats to it.

2. Interventionist Theism

The position I am calling Interventionist Theism is a position many people take to be the standard understanding of the God-world relation in Christianity. At the same time, there are complications regarding just what is implied by this position, even

[5] ST 1 49.

when it is regarded as the standard one, and I comment on some of those complications while presenting the position.

In general, this position regards God as a supernatural being who is "out there," separate from the world. As in Deism, God is regarded as creator of the world. Unlike Deism, God is regarded as having more of an intimate relationship with the world. Following the biblical tradition, God is pictured very much in personal terms. God is a supernatural person existing in a realm alongside the world who carries out a historical plan for the world. Deism was a new belief system that emerged in Western Christianity in the modern period. Interventionist Theism flourished alongside Deism in the modern period and into our own day.

Insofar as Interventionist Theism is a Christian interpretation, the Old and New Testaments were regarded as giving the story of God's interaction with the world. At the risk of being simplistic, we can summarize this story. God chooses the Jewish people to be God's special agents in history to enact the divine plan for the world. This plan includes entering into a covenant with the Jews and giving them the covenant law. God continues to be faithful to the covenant through the ups and downs of Jewish history, including their establishing of a nation and eventually their political defeat and exile. Finally, at the right time, God becomes incarnate in the person of Jesus. Jesus' death and resurrection shows the defeat of the powers of sin, suffering, and death in the universe by God. This occurs in the middle of history. Jesus ascends to God's right hand and awaits the appointed time at the end of history when he will return and establish a new heaven and new earth without sin, suffering, and death under God's rule. In the meantime, the Christian church lives acknowledging and participating in the victory over sin, suffering, and death brought about by Jesus' death and resurrection, and anticipating the future defeat of them in the coming Kingdom of God.

One of the complications of this understanding of the God-world relation involves the question whether God made the world so that it runs on its own, as Deists affirm, or whether God's active powers are somehow involved in upholding the world at all times. If one affirms the latter, then one breaks with Deism about an important aspect of the God-world relation. Yet another complication has to do with the question of just how God relates to the world in carrying out God's plan. Does God work through human freedom and the ordinary operation of reality in carrying out God's plan at least most of the time? Was that true in the biblical period and is it still true today?

However, these latter questions are answered, this position is called Interventionist Theism because at some key point or points it is understood that God directly intervenes in the causal process we experience as a discrete cause. God is a powerful being alongside the universe. God made the universe and its laws, so God can break those laws and intervene in the universe to carry out God's plan. The Old and New Testaments are full of examples of these interventions and violations of natural laws. Focusing on the New Testament alone, Jesus is born of a virgin while a miraculous astrological event bears witness to his messianic status and Divine messengers provide secret knowledge to protect him in his infancy (Mt 1:18-2:23). Jesus shows his power over demonic forces by casting out demons from possessed people. He heals people suffering from illness and disability, including raising two people from the dead (Mk 5:21-43, Jn 11:1-44). He does nature miracles, providing food for people and calming storms. After being crucified, he is himself resurrected, and while his resurrection appearances are often mysterious, he is presented with a definite body that can be touched and that either needs to eat or is simply capable of eating (Lk 24:36-43, Jn 20:24-29). After a brief period that involves a series of appearances, Jesus ascends to heaven to be with

God, while his followers are told he will come back in the same way that he left (Acts 1:6-11).

All of these interventions presuppose a picture of God as a powerful personal being in a realm above enacting a plan on earth below. This picture has operated effectively throughout Christian history, giving assurance of Divine care and of the fact that human history and human destiny are in God's hands. For many people in the modern and contemporary period, it can be accepted immediately and without questioning. For others, elements of this worldview have become unbelievable and even outlandish. Given what we know about the universe, do we really expect Jesus to return as the Son of Man on the clouds of heaven, send out his angels, and gather his elect? Do we have to accept the virgin birth as a biological fact or that astrological manipulations and inside information from Divine messengers accompanied that birth? Must we believe that Jesus had a literal resurrected body?

It must be stressed that for many Christians, the very fact of raising these questions seems unacceptable and damaging. The Bible and its message is a Divine authority. It speaks and has a power as nothing else in the world. Questioning what the Bible says in this fundamental way, a way that does not just seek out what the Bible means but asks whether the biblical claims could possibly be true, is equated with questioning God. To do this means to lose faith and fall outside the supporting and upholding power of belief in God. However, it remains the case that for others in the modern world and into the present, this questioning is unavoidable. It is the consequence of our cultural situation in which autonomous thinking has emerged. The emergence of autonomous thinking brought with it the power to criticize the Bible and religious authorities. Such criticism is not regarded as faithlessness or rebelliousness. It is an expression of a sincere desire for knowledge or truth.

There are many ways in which the kind of critical questioning of the Bible mentioned above can be justified, but at least one major way points to the fact that our understanding of any period of history is rooted in our understanding of how reality works in the present.[6] Every historical moment is unique, but the conditions by which each moment of the past can be understood must be based on an analogy with our understanding of how reality works now. This means our current grasp of the world through the natural sciences, social sciences, history, and philosophy are all relevant for understanding recorded biblical history and can rightly be brought into a critical relationship with our understanding of that history. In other words, for example, it is not adequate to claim that Greek mythology or the Hindu stories about the Gods are clearly false and we can criticize them on the basis of our understanding of the world today, but the biblical story cannot be criticized on that basis. It is also not adequate to claim, for example, that the many miraculous events recorded in the Bible occurred just like the Bible says, but that was a special time different from our own. In our own time, we cannot expect those things to occur. Reality is one. We understand the past on the basis of how we understand reality to work now and we can and must criticize alternative understandings of the past that contradict that understanding.

Tillich thought autonomous thinking needed to be given full sway and that meant the Bible and church teaching could not be exempt from critical questioning. To do theology in our day and age means accepting this. He regarded the desire to exempt the

---

[6] A notable thinker that takes this position in articulating the philosophical bases of historical knowledge is Ernst Troeltsch. See his essay from 1898, "Historical and Dogmatic Method in Theology," in *Religion in History*, trans. James Luther Adams and Walter F. Bense (Minneapolis: Fortress Press, 1991).

Bible from critical questioning and affirm that its literal descriptions of miraculous events must have occurred as an expression of what he called "heteronomy." Heteronomy literally means "other law." In this sense, it is the opposite of autonomy, which is self-law or the law of reason. In a heteronomous cultural situation, some external beliefs are imposed upon the self. These beliefs make the claim of being ultimate truth or Divine truth. They are affirmed in the name of God. But they come to the subject as something alien to and in conflict with the subject's own autonomous reflection. They demand a choice: accept the truths of critical thinking and reject Divine truth or accept Divine truth and reject the truths of critical thinking. Such a choice is ultimately destructive for the subject. One must sacrifice either the integrity of knowing or a relation to the Divine.

In a dramatic use of language, Tillich often uses the term "demonic," to refer to the demand to accept some particular truth or truths as Divine truths. In the New Testament context, the belief in supernatural beings called demons was commonplace. Demons were thought to have the capacity of taking over someone's personal center, and in so doing they broke down that center, ruining people's lives. In the same way, for Tillich, the demand to accept some supernatural truths when they conflict with the authentic quest for knowledge or the right way to act, is a demand requiring the destruction of one's personal center. It is demonic in the sense that one is compelled to accept something supernatural, but what one accepts is something that destroys the self rather than healing and integrating the self.

We can develop Tillich's critique of heteronomy in relation to different fields of knowledge and apply it to contemporary examples. I have already given the example that the requirement of belief in biblical miracles would be considered heteronomous to Tillich. In relation to the natural sciences, Tillich would certainly claim that the rejection of an old earth, the acceptance of a global flood as having explanatory scientific meaning, and the rejection of biological evolution through natural selection on the basis of a literal reading of the Bible would all be examples of demonic heteronomy. They are destructive impositions on autonomous knowing in the supposed name of Divine truth. They emerge from the idea that God is a being alongside the universe whose Word is absolute and is spoken in a literal way in the biblical text.

From a Tillichian perspective, taking a position on some complex moral issue like abortion, or the set of issues surrounding gay and lesbian rights, on the basis of a literal reading of biblical verses would also be an example of heteronomy. Basing one's position on certain biblical passages means absolutizing a text with its cultural norms from the past as Divine truth rather than giving autonomous ethical thinking the space and consideration it deserves in ethical decision making.

Throughout his career, Tillich spoke adamantly against explicitly religious heteronomy. It can be defined as the failure to regard a religious symbol as a symbol and instead literalizing the symbol and regarding it as absolute. Examples of this include the absolutization of a cultic system, and regarding participation in that system as the only way of establishing a right relationship with God. He interpreted the Hebrew prophets' critique of the priestly cult in the name of the God of justice as a prime example of the legitimate critique of heteronomy.[7] He also interpreted the Protestant critique of the Roman Catholic sacramental system in the name of internal forgiveness and transformation of life as an

[7] Consider this potent quote from the Prophet Amos (God is speaking): "I hate, I despise your festivals, and I take no delight in your solemn assemblies. Even though you offer me your burnt offerings and grain offerings, I will not accept them; and the offerings of well-being of your fatted animals I will not look upon. Take away from me the noise of your songs; I will not listen to the melody of your harps. But let justice roll down like waters, and righteousness like an ever-flowing stream" (Amos 5:21-24).

example of the legitimate critique of heteronomy. Famously, Tillich coined the term "Protestant Principle" to refer to the protest against identifying God with any hierarchical body or sacramental system.[8]

Tillich's anti-heteronomy analysis can be applied to the discussion about patriarchal language for God that has emerged in the decades since his death.[9] With the feminist movement's push for female equality, Christian feminists noted that calling God "Father, Lord, and King" reinforces male power because these terms of patriarchal authority are invested with Divine meaning. In Tillich's terms, since a symbol participates in that to which it points, it is male leadership that participates in Divine power and rule. Clinging to these patriarchal symbols would be, in a Tillichean analysis, demonic heteronomy, since it reinforces male rule and, with this, suppresses the autonomous emergence of female authority. From a Tillichian perspective, it is also the case that one should expect resistance to the critique and transformation of this patriarchal language, since, as symbols, they are concrete ways in which God is experienced. Questioning them could certainly appear to be questioning God.

Finally, anti-heteronomy analysis can and should be applied to the issue of interreligious relations. A Tillichean approach to interreligious relations would critique any individual religious group's claim that it alone relates to God while other groups do not, the root of such a claim being that God exists alongside the

---

[8] See especially the "Author's Introduction" in PE for Tillich's description of the Protestant Principle.

[9] Classic works of Christian feminist theology that criticize the exclusive use of male language for God include Rosemary Radford Ruether, *Sexism and God-Talk: Toward a Feminist Theology* (Boston: Beacon Press, 1983), Sallie McFague, *Models of God: Theology for an Ecological Nuclear Age* (Minneapolis: Fortress Press, 1987), and Elizabeth Johnson, *She Who Is: The Mystery of God in Feminist Theological Discourse* (Crossroads Pub. Co. 1992).

world and has revealed God's self to one group of people while excluding others. For Tillich, people of all religious traditions relate to the same ultimate reality. They do this in different concrete ways and through differing, though often overlapping, concrete symbols. The beginning of any understanding of another religious tradition must proceed from the position of respect other traditions deserve as an individual realization of relatedness to what is universal.[10]

3. Panentheism

The understanding of the relationship between God and the world, where the infinite upholds, pervades, and transcends the finite, is sometimes called "panentheism." Although Tillich himself never used the term, it appears to express his position. The term literally means "everything is in God." It has elements in common with what is often called "pantheism." Pantheism simply means "everything is God." As Tillich points out repeatedly, pantheists are not so naïve as to affirm that every individual object in the world is literally God. Put this way, it just sounds silly. God is not literally this desk, computer, or pencil. In pantheism, however, God is conceived as an essential, ever-present reality in, to, and pulsating through the finite world. In this sense, everything is God, because God is present in, to, and through all things. However, at least in some understandings of pantheism, God does not

---

[10] This is not to suggest that Tillich was a pluralist in the sense that he regarded all religious traditions as different but nevertheless equal mediators of the Divine presence. Throughout his work, Tillich argued for a variety of criteria to determine religious truth and he consistently claimed that the events on which Christianity was based fulfilled those criteria in the highest degree. A nuanced analysis of Tillich's approach to religious traditions other than Christianity can be found in Robison James, *Tillich and World Religions: Encountering other Faiths Today* (Macon Georgia: Mercer University Press, 2003).

transcend or go beyond the whole of the world. God is ultimately identified with the whole of the world. Tillich clearly rejects this latter idea. For Tillich, God is that which is infinite, absolute, and unconditioned. God pervades the finite but can never be limited by it.

Tillich denies that God can be rightly conceived as a being with attributes alongside the world. With this, he rejects both deism and interventionist theism. Against Deism, for Tillich, part of what is involved in grasping the depth of the relationship between God and the world is grasping the fact that the finite is not self-sustaining. The world is not like a top that has been set spinning or a car that has been started and is running on its own. It has an infinite ground within it, or, better put, the infinite ground contains finitude within itself. Against Interventionist Theism, Tillich claims an idea of God as a discrete cause alongside the universe who intervenes in it from time to time both violates God's transcendence of finite causality and invariably leads to heteronomy.

What is Tillich's alternative to what he regards as a shallow autonomy and an oppressive heteronomy? He calls it "theonomy." Theonomy means "God's law." It is a cultural situation in which all autonomous activity is open to its depths or to being-itself or the ground of meaning. All cultural activity is done as an expression of and in openness to the ultimate meaningfulness that pulsates through every articulation of meaning.

For Tillich, the way in which autonomous activity stays open to its ground, and the way in which it is healed when it becomes distorted, is through keeping religion alive in the culture. Religion is a direct relation to the unconditioned. Culture relates to the unconditioned only indirectly and is constantly prone to losing its connection. When religion is active in a culture without being heteronomous but enabling further deep realizations of autonomy, then theonomy is realized. In theonomy, both religion and autonomous culture that is open to its depths thrive.

In Tillich's interpretation, no situation is every fully theonomous, just as no situation is ever merely autonomous or merely heteronomous. These categories are tendencies that emerge in various historical epochs. In our own time, in one of Tillich's articulations of intellectual history, autonomy emerged with the breakthrough of modernity. It became shallow, pushing God into the distance and seeking especially to understand those aspects of reality that can be measured and calculated through the natural sciences and then applying the knowledge gained in technology and industry. With the postulate of God no longer needed to understand the world, atheism was the consequence. In the human focus on grasping only calculable and measurable reality, humans finally dehumanized themselves, turning themselves into calculable objects. The reaction against this came, among other ways, in atheistic existentialism. It represents a kind of despairing reaction against dehumanization.[11]

This cultural situation played itself out in face of what was often a heteronomous reaction from Christian churches. One of the primary forms of this reaction in Tillich's analysis is a denial of knowledge for the sake of "faith." Throughout his career, Tillich was critical of an understanding of faith that regarded faith as an inferior kind of knowledge that was supposed to be held with such passion that it was able to overcome the contradictions between what it affirms about reality and what the sciences and history affirm about reality.[12] Faith cannot contradict reason. If it tries to do so, it becomes reactionary and anti-rational. It is demonic and destructive.

---

[11] This analysis is prominent in CB 131-154.

[12] DF 30-40.

Autonomy tends toward blindness and because of this it can be destructive. Heteronomy tends toward oppression and because of this it can be destructive. Based on a reading of the cultural situation outlined above, Tillich called for a new theonomy that overcomes the limitations of autonomy and heteronomy. Theonomy cannot be created in a strict sense, or in the same way a new kind of technology can be created by using the right materials and knowledge. Theonomy has to emerge. Its emergence would signify what Tillich called a "Kairos" in history. Kairos refers to a pregnant moment or a full moment. It is a moment in which something new can burst forth and provide a historical turning point. The bursting forth of a new theonomy is never complete and never perfect. It is, however, for Tillich, always possible because both religion and culture are based on the ground of being that has the power to ever renew creation. It is never clear in advance precisely how this renewal will take place, but the infinite ground has within it the capacity to endlessly bring about something new in every religio-cultural context.

Chapter 4

Openings to the Awareness of God

How do we know there is a God, let alone a God like the one Tillich affirms?

As it is traditionally expressed, the question of proving the "existence" of God is a question that blossomed in vitality and importance in the modern world. Arguably, that vitality and importance remain with us today.

There is no serious questioning about whether or not there is a God in the Bible, nor are proofs given for God's existence. Famously, the first verse of the Jewish and Christian Bible does not try to prove there is a God but presupposes God's existence and announces God's activity in creating the world. It is true that the Psalmist says, "The heavens declare the glory of God" (Psalms 19:1), but this is an acclamation, not a proof. All of the ancient Near Eastern cultures around Israel believed in God or the Gods and none of them developed rigorous proofs for their beliefs.

At the time of the New Testament, Jews believed in their God, and Romans had temples dedicated to their many deities throughout the Roman Empire. There were so many temples and so many deities, in fact, that the Gospel of Acts records the Apostle Paul referring to a temple to an unknown God in the city of

Athens – just in case they left one out (Acts 17:23)! Jesus was never concerned with giving a proof that God exists. His mission was to tell people about God's coming kingdom and what to do to prepare for it (Mk 1:14-15). Paul probably comes as close to a proof as there is in the New Testament. He says in Romans, "Ever since the creation of the world [God's] eternal power and divine nature, invisible though they are, have been understood and seen through the things he has made..." (1:20a). This is not an actual proof, however, for Paul never gives an argument for how God's eternal power and divine nature are understood and seen through creation. He just asserts that they are.[1]

Given the universal belief in God in the ancient world, the theologians of the early church apparently saw no need to prove that the God revealed in Jewish history, and, to them, most fully in Jesus, existed. They sought to clarify what belief in Jesus meant, and to defend the validity of that belief to the outside world. It is only deep in the Middle Ages in the West, where we see rigorous proofs for God's existence emerge, most famously in the works of Anselm of Canterbury (1033-1109) and Thomas Aquinas (1225-1274). Even here, however, both thinkers made it clear that their proofs were not required for faith. Both men's proofs were debated in their own time and after, not by atheists and non-believers, but by other Christians who disagreed with the validity of their reasoning or their approach. In fact, famously, Thomas rejected An-

---

[1] This passage where Paul seems to suggest humans can know God through creation can and often is exegeted in such a way as to suggest that Paul is referring to human beings in their "original" condition before the fall into sin and not their actual condition after the fall into sin. According to this exegesis, in the totality of this passage in Romans 1, Paul is claiming that in their actual condition, humans minds are so warped that they cannot know the true God who would or could have been known through creation had humans not fallen from their original condition.

selm's proof while giving his own. Even if a proof for God's existence was thought to be valid, no one in the Middle Ages thought belief in God ultimately rested on such a proof. Belief in God rested on the authority of church teaching.

The situation changed with the emergence of the Enlightenment and modern ways of thinking. As explained in chapter three, the Enlightenment elevated human reason, or autonomous human knowing. It also involved a daring critique of the authorities of the church (the Bible, church hierarchy, traditional church teaching) and the state (the divine right of the Monarch to rule).

In this context, proofs for the existence of God acquired new significance. When reason mattered more, the proofs mattered more. If someone is to live according to what their reason tells them, does it tell them God exists or not? If it does, a religion grounded in reason is possible. If it does not, then what? Can you will yourself to believe in something rationally unprovable? Should you abandon belief in God and look for explanations of that belief in non-rational factors? These are enormous questions that become tenable in the modern period.

As the proofs for God's existence gained significance in the modern period, new articulations of the proofs were put forward even as new rounds of critiques followed. The most famous modern critics of the proofs were David Hume (1711-1776), in his *Dialogues Concerning Natural Religion*, and Immanuel Kant (1724-1804), in his *Critique of Pure Reason*. The standing of the proofs from Hume and Kant's time forward—who believed them, who did not, which proofs, and why—is a complex part of intellectual history. Beneath the complexity, however, one can trace the eventual emergence of a culturally respectable atheism in the West that is a distinctive feature of the contemporary period. While there may have been hidden atheists in the Middle Ages, the period of the Protestant Reformation, and the early modern period, there was no culturally acceptable space for them. In our own time, without question, atheism is one of the worldviews embraced by some reflective people in the West. One would certainly have to say that among the many factors leading to the emergence of atheism as a legitimate option is the elevation in significance of the proofs for the existence of God and, in particular, the power of the critiques against those proofs.

While the traditional proofs for God's existence and their critiques have had and continue to have a role to play in our current cultural situation, numerous thinkers have also sought alternative ways of doing theology that neither relied on the traditional proofs nor resorted to a shallow fideism.[2] Tillich stands in this development. As Tillich repeatedly points out, the alternative approach that he follows goes back at least to the Protestant theologian Friedrich Schleiermacher (1768-1834), who is considered by many Protestants the father of modern theology.[3] While Tillich gives credence to the historical importance of the proofs, in choosing to follow another way of doing theology, he often critiques the proofs vigorously. This chapter examines his critique, the reasons for it, and the distinctive elements of his alternative approach.

---

[2] "Fideism" means to accept a set of beliefs by faith without reason, arguments, or proofs for those beliefs.

[3] Like Tillich, Schleiermacher was a philosopher, a theoretician of religion, and a Christian theologian. One of his most important early works on religious theory is *On Religion: Speeches to its Cultured Despisers* (Cambridge: Cambridge University Press, 1988). In this work, he describes religion as a "sense and taste for the infinite." Also like Tillich, his main work of systematic theology, called *The Christian Faith* (Edinburgh: T and T Clark, 1989), combines religious theory or philosophy of religion and theology. In this work he defines the essence of religion as a "feeling of absolute dependence."

1. Proofs for God's existence do not work because God does not exist

As stated earlier, famously among contemporary theologians and philosophers of religion, Tillich strongly affirms that God does not exist. Tillich does not claim this in order to negate the idea or reality of God, but to affirm the absoluteness of God. God is that which is most real about reality. To call God another being, to put God into another realm, to claim God is another substance or cause, is to apply finite categories to God and negate God's absoluteness. God does not exist. God is being-itself, or the ground and power of being. Everything that exists, does so in and because of God. God does not exist in and because of anything.

With this background in mind, it is easy to see why Tillich critiques the arguments for God's existence: they have the wrong goal. They seek to show that a supernatural being with certain properties exists alongside or beyond the world, and, for Tillich, no such being exists. Paradoxically for a Christian theologian, the critiques of the arguments for God's existence are actually helpful for Tillich's argument. In showing that the arguments for God's existence do not work, the critiques open up the possibility that the God of the arguments is not the true God.

At times, Tillich critiques the arguments for their wrong-headed idea of God in dramatic language, stating, for example, "…to argue that God exists is to deny him."[4] He means by this that the process of trying to prove the existence of a supernatural being beyond the world misses or denies the real God. Sometimes he explicitly credits atheism with providing a positive function for Christian theology. It helps negate the false idea of God as a supernatural being alongside the world.[5]

---

[4] *ST* I, 205.

[5] See, for example, ST I 245 and TC 5.

Along with having the wrong goal, there is another and perhaps deeper element in Tillich's critique of the traditional arguments. Tillich lambasts their method, or the way they approach the question of God's existence. The most common of the traditional arguments for God's existence are what are called empirical arguments.[6] They begin with the assumption that God and humans are separated. Because of this separation, it is meaningful to say that God may or may not exist. Whether God exists is something humans do not know. What humans do know is the world given to us through our senses. Using our reason, we are able to discern certain features of the world, things like causality, contingency, and order. The arguments for God's existence, then, proceed to claim that these features of the world are not self-explained. They can only be explained by positing the existence of a supernatural being beyond the world that accounts for them.

It is this approach in particular that Tillich blames for the emergence of disbelief in God. This approach involves denying an immediate, universal, and inherent relationship between humans and God. It makes the claim that we only experience the world and must use a reasoning process to reach God who may or may not exist beyond the world. In face of what Tillich regards as the error of this approach, he proposes his own way of affirming the reality of God. In his way, it is not that the world alone is experienced, and God is a questionable object that may or may not exist beyond the world, a conclusion to be reached through a reasoning process. Instead, the Divine reality imposes itself on the human

---

[6] This is true of what are traditionally called the cosmological and teleological arguments, though not the ontological argument. While he does not think the ontological argument works as an argument, Tillich does say positive things about it that he does not say about the other traditional arguments. See TC, 15-16.

subject at all times. It is not just the world, but God who is constantly present to us. What we need to do is look in the right way in order to be aware of God's presence.

2. The Awareness of God in Knowing and Doing

Tillich commonly uses the term "unconditioned" or "the unconditioned" to refer to God. It is an appropriate term for Tillich's conception of God because it points to something the mind cannot grasp. In our ordinary experience of the world, as well as in the most intense scientific quest for knowledge, the mind conditions objects with its concepts and categories. Put differently, as described in chapter one, the mind and objects come together to make knowledge possible. However, the infinite, ultimate, or absolute cannot be conditioned by the mind. It is owing to God's greatness and surpassing reality that God remains unconditioned. The problem, of course, is how we can know something that is unconditioned. To Tillich, none of the categories we apply to the finite world can be applied literally to God and we cannot reason to God as a being alongside the world based on some inexplicable features of the world. So how can we know God?

First of all, to Tillich, in an important sense, we cannot know God. Tillich would want us never to lose sight of this. Knowledge is the unity of subject and object through concepts and categories. God is not a possible object alongside the world of which we would have a corresponding concept. To think of God in this way is to denigrate God and subject God to some aspect of the world. However, while we cannot know God, according to Tillich, we can have what he commonly calls an "awareness" of God.

The awareness of God, or of something infinite or unconditioned, for Tillich, always accompanies our awareness of objects. It is always there, even if we do not pay attention to it. This means that like our awareness of the world, the awareness of God is immediate. In our conscious experience, our minds condition reality immediately. Except perhaps in cases of drunkenness or stupor, the world given to us through the senses is grasped by our minds in an immediate way. It is in this same immediacy that an awareness of God is given or present.

God, or the unconditioned, that is given in immediacy is not another object. Instead, Tillich says, the unconditioned is present as "an element, a power, as demand."[7] God is the ground of all being. This, of course, includes human life and human reality. As we described in chapter two, for Tillich, humans have the most being of all beings we know. Humans are not simply subject to the laws of matter in motion nor do they relate to their environment merely through instinct. Humans are free and fully self-conscious. We create lives of meaning through this freedom and self-awareness. All human cultures with their modes and transmission of knowledge, aesthetic expression, and forms of communal life that strive for justice and love are creations of meaning. We live in these worlds of meaning. It is in them that the unconditioned must appear immediately as an element, power, and demand.

Tillich expends significant effort in his work describing the appearance of the unconditioned in all realms of cultural life. In an important sense, this broad description of the unconditioned in culture serves as his primary proof for the reality of God.[8] Chapter six covers in depth Tillich's analysis of the way in which God, or the unconditioned, appears in culture. However, when Tillich focuses in particular on *evidence* for the presence of the unconditioned in human life, which is his more direct equivalent of proofs

---

[7] *TC* 23.

[8] Tillich also affirms that the unconditioned can be recognized in the natural world (TC 27). This recognition of the unconditioned in the inorganic, organic, and animal realms gives to all of life its "greatness" (ST III 88-92).

for the existence of God, he tends to focus on the key human activities of knowing and doing, with the latter emphasizing ethical doing. Human knowing, or human cognition of the world, and human ethical actions in relation to each other are so fundamental to human life that Tillich turns especially to them for evidence of the presence of the unconditioned.

For the unconditioned to be present in knowing and ethical action means that an awareness of the ground of those activities must appear in them. As Tillich explains, insofar as the unconditioned appears in human knowing, it appears as the presence of truth-itself in the mind. Insofar as the unconditioned appears in ethical action, it appears as the presence of goodness-itself in the mind. Truth-itself is the unconditioned ground or basis of all true judgments about reality. It is what makes true judgments possible. Goodness-itself is the unconditioned ground or basis of all good acts in relation to reality. It is what makes good acts possible.[9]

Tillich credits Augustine of Hippo (354-430) as being the Christian theologian who most clearly shows the indelible presence of truth-itself in the mind. Tillich explains that Augustine confronted ancient skepticism about the possibility of finding truth by showing that truth-itself is present and presupposed in every judgment. Tillich never unfolds Augustine's argument in detail, nor does he develop it in anything but a suggestive way. Much of what I say in explaining it expands on Tillich's suggestions.[10]

Knowing always involves the unity of subject and object. Truth-itself is neither the knowing subject nor an object known but the basis or the ground of the subject-object unity in knowing.

---

[9] ST I 206-207.

[10] The argument Tillich follows from Augustine is stated in his *Soliloquies* (In *Augustine: Earlier Writings*, Philadelphia: Westminster Press, 1953) 23-63. Tillich's statements about Augustine's argument can be found in TC, 12-13; and ST 1, 206-207.

This ground determines the subject's activity in its grasp of reality. We make judgments about our grasp of reality all the time. We want to know the truth of what we experience. Is my grasp of reality accurate? Is that water on the road ahead or does it just look that way? It sure seems like the sun goes around the earth, but does it? Science is the rigorous approach to reality that seeks the proper methods to assure the validity or truth of our grasp of reality at all levels. The emergence of science, which seeks to know the whole of reality, is one way of showing that human knowing is driven by an unconditioned demand to know. We do not and cannot cut off knowing in any realm. And science insists on pursuing truth with honesty. The scientific method denies the option of fudging the facts for personal convenience. While biases certainly may influence knowing, to follow one's biases is not knowing but a violation of it. Science is driven by an unconditioned demand not only to know everything but to know things as they are, apart from personal whim. This unconditioned demand is the operation of the ground of knowing in the subject in the process of knowing.

It is possible for someone who seeks knowledge to be frustrated in the attempt to find it. Reality is confounding. It does not always give itself to us easily. In the midst of the quest for knowledge, someone may claim, "there is no truth." Such a statement, however, reinstates truth since it makes a claim to be true. The very attempt to deny all knowledge reinstates knowledge in a way that shows there must be a ground of unity between the knowing subject and the objects known.

When one claims, "there is no truth," one is claiming that the mind is unable to grasp reality or that the subject cannot grasp objects. However, in that claim, there is an underlying assumption that one knows and can make a judgment about the relationship between the mind and reality. This is why one reinstates truth in the complete denial of truth. In the claim "there is no truth," one claims the relationship between the mind and reality is a disrelationship, a breach, or a break. However, to know there is this breach or break between mind and reality assumes the operation of a ground, basis, or link between mind and reality. This basis, link, or ground is truth-itself appearing in the mind. It is not the truth of some particular piece of knowing or some proposition about reality. It is the basis of all knowing or all propositions about reality. It is not something that the mind can condition and know. Rather, it is that which conditions the mind in its relation to reality. It is the mind's own ground involved in all knowing, all grasping of reality. To use another image, it is the light shining in the mind and on all objects that the mind is aware of and that makes knowing possible. The mind cannot turn around, as it were, and look at the light, but the mind is aware that it is there because it cannot deny its own ground that makes knowing possible.

The indelibility of the ground of the unity between subject and object makes absolute skepticism about our knowing impossible. We must be able to know because our attempt to deny it utterly reinstates or presupposes the fact that there must be a ground of unity between subject and object. In this way, truth-itself as the ground of the unity between subject and object is the basis of all knowing and all of the sciences. It is present in every act of knowing. It is the possibility of knowing and the norm of knowing. Whenever someone says "is that judgment true? Let's look further and find out!" that person is operating according to the presence of the norm of truth in the mind.

Tillich credits Immanuel Kant (1724-1804) as being the philosopher who most clearly shows the indelible presence of goodness itself in our ethical actions. Famously, in Kant's ethics, Kant develops what he called the "categorical imperative."[11] In Tillichian language, it could appropriately be called the "unconditional imperative."

As Tillich interprets Kant, if we look at the basis of our ethical actions in relation to ourselves and others, we find the presence of something unconditioned that makes a demand on us. This unconditioned demand is immediately present in all ethical reasoning or any time a person asks how they should act in relation to themselves or another person. It is not derived from the situation, but is a presupposition of every situation that calls for ethical action. It is there despite how a person may feel or someone's individual desires or whims. It cannot be derived from any goal a person may have owing to the given situation in which that person finds him or herself. Independent of conditions, when we reason about how we should act in relation to ourselves and others, we discover an unconditional imperative. This, in Tillich's interpretation, is the presence of goodness-itself in the mind.

The presence and influence of goodness-itself is not another good action. It makes demands on all actions. One cannot argue to it on the basis of a given situation since it is present and determinative in every situation where ethical reasoning holds sway. In this way, it is something immediately given with our actions rather than derived from them.

Kant gave several formulations of the categorical imperative. The two most notable ones are that you should act so that the basis by which you act can be a universal law, and you should act so that you do not simply treat yourself or others as a means but

---

[11] The two works in which Kant develops his ethical theory most comprehensively are *Foundations of the Metaphysics of Morals* (New York: Macmillan, 1959), originally published in 1785, and *Critique of Practical Reason* (New York: Macmillan, 1956), originally published in 1788.

as an end in itself.[12] What is important to Tillich is not whether these formulations, or perhaps others, entirely encapsulate the imperative. He is not concerned with the nitty-gritty debates of the formulations of the imperative or how these formulations may or may not be applied to individual cases. His concern and his crediting of Kant is in the uncovering of the presence of the imperative as an unconditional demand in all ethical activity.

While Tillich credits Augustine and Kant for being the two figures in Western intellectual history who most clearly bring to the fore the insight into the presence of the unconditioned in knowing and ethical action, he also faults them both for going beyond their analysis of the presence of the unconditioned as element, presence, and demand. Both thinkers, says Tillich, attempt to turn the unconditioned into something that exists, or an unconditional being within reality.[13] Their analysis is accurate, insofar as they uncover the presence of something unconditioned in knowing and doing. Their thinking is faulty insofar as each tries to extend what should be the awareness of an unconditioned element in human experience into the affirmation of the determined existence of an unconditioned being within reality.

For Tillich, human beings and God are indelibly linked. This link is presupposed in our knowing and ethical activity. To describe the knowing process and ethical activity in such a way as to disclose this link is what functions as a proof for the reality of God. It is not the kind of proof that attempts to show that something unknown (God) must exist because of what we know (the world). It is a disclosure showing that human knowing and ethical activity are rooted in human's link with God.

---

[12] Both are stated in *Foundations of the Metaphysics of Morals* (New York: Macmillan, 1959) 39,47.

[13] ST I 207.

Chapter 5

The God of Religion

The realm of religion involves a host of traditions that display a mind-boggling array of practices. Christianity, for example, promotes a weekly worship service. Most services involve singing, prayer, and preaching, and, depending on the denomination, services may or may not involve celebration of the Eucharist. Between Christian denominations, there are major debates about the correct form of worship. Some denominations have formal services and follow a standard liturgy every week. Other denominations' services are more informal and attendees are given considerable space to speak and pray what comes into their hearts and minds at the moment. The worship spaces of some denominations are filled with religious images or statues. Other denominations' worship spaces are sparse, with perhaps the only visible religious object being a cross.

Many religious traditions do not promote weekly worship services. People may attend formal or informal services of various kinds on an as-needed or as-desired basis, or for significant moments in their lives or the lives of family members. Yet other traditions eschew prayer directed to a God who is conceived personally. Some promote meditation practices, which themselves can vary widely in rigor, technique, and articulated goal. Still others regard things like pilgrimages to sacred sites as significant. Such pilgrimages may involve bathing in a sacred river or climbing a sacred mountain.

Given the teeming variety of religious beliefs and practices, can we make sense of religion in any theoretical way? Can we develop categories to understand religious beliefs and practices in terms of their goal, the structural character of religious objects, and some common attitude or approach that is characteristic of religious devotees? This is a task for the philosophy of religion. Tillich thinks the philosophy of religion can and must work out such a theoretical construction and he offers one in his work.

The alternative to a theoretical construction for understanding religious phenomena would be to claim that religion is a major aspect of human life displayed throughout all of human history whose meaning we simply cannot understand.[1] Ultimately, we would have to put each religious tradition in a separate box, claim that each one is doing something different and baffling, and leave it at that.[2]

---

[1] There is also the reductionistic position that claims religion emerges from and can be reduced to non-religious sources. Options include the claim that religion is the projection of a father-image rooted in fear (Freud), it is a mind-numbing drug that keeps the masses from coming to terms with their economic oppression (Marx), and it is the tool of the weak to keep the strong in check (Nietzsche). Variants of these claims manifest themselves in versions of modern atheism.

[2] This view is sometimes called "particularism." One notable attempt to provide a theoretical justification of particularism is in George Lindbeck, *The Nature of Doctrine* (Philadelphia: Westminster Press, 1984). Lindbeck claims there is no common relatedness to ultimate reality that is expressed in a variety of ways in different religious traditions. Instead, individuals in each religious tradition have the religious experiences they have because they are shaped and formed by that religious tradition. The religious tradition creates the religious experience of individuals and each experience in each tradition is decidedly different. This view is widely critiqued for hopelessly separating

In truth, such an approach is appealing to some Christians as well as some devotees of other religious traditions. If each religious tradition is separate and theoretically incomprehensible, it opens the possibility that one's own tradition is the place where the true revelation from God is found. If we can categorically understand religion, then every religious tradition is in some significant sense brought to the same level. This does not mean abandoning all criteria for determining what constitutes legitimate or illegitimate religious acts, but it does mean that everyone relates to the same ultimate reality only in different ways. Religion, understood as a way of relating to the infinite, is universal.

Tillich makes a strong argument for the universality of religion. Religion is so vital, so potent, and so significant in human history and human life everywhere that it cannot be understood as having dropped from heaven in a true form in one place while being false everywhere else. It is a structural component of human life and the failure to understand it as such is to blind oneself to an understanding of human life. It is also the case that from a religious point of view, any God who would limit God's revelation to one special group seems arbitrary and unjust.

I present Tillich's analysis of religion in this chapter, focusing on religious symbols and their meaning for Tillich's understanding of God, Tillich's conceptuality of the inner dynamics of religion, and the religious orientation and its meaning for the human relation to God.

---

the religious traditions from one another and for being a theoretical ruse for affirming the exclusive superiority of one's own tradition.

1. Symbols as a Fusion of the Ultimate and the Concrete

For Tillich, religion involves an immediate relation to what is conceived as ultimate. He never loses sight of the immediacy or immediate encounter with the Divine that is part of all religious traditions. All religions involve practices of some kind. As stated above, options include worship, prayer, song, meditation, and pilgrimages. For Tillich, these are ways in which humans come into direct relationship with the Divine presence or some ultimate power.

The complication, of course, is accounting for the wide variety of ways the Divine presence is conceived among the different religions in the history of humankind. Tillich attempts to account for this variety with his theory of religious symbols, a theory initially introduced in chapter two and expanded upon here.

To understand Tillich's theory of symbols, we must reiterate the point that for Tillich we do not and cannot have literal language to refer to God. God is the ultimate, infinite, absolute, or unconditioned. We have concepts and categories that refer to the finite world that enable us to grasp and understand that world, but we do not have concepts and categories that apply to what is ultimate or unconditioned. If this is the case, how can there be a direct relation with God, which is the essence of religion? For Tillich, it occurs through symbols.

The first point to be made, then, about religious symbols is that they are living mediators of the Divine presence. They are concrete ways by which devotees experience God. As stated in chapter two, Tillich says symbols and signs have the feature in common of pointing to something beyond themselves with the difference between them being that signs are arbitrary pointers and can theoretically be changed, whereas symbols, in Tillich's language, "participate" in that to which they point.[3] By claiming a symbol participates in that to which it points, he means symbols mediate or make present what is ultimately beyond them. At one point, he says a religious symbol "participates in the power of the divine to which it points."[4] Ultimacy or infinity is experienced through the symbol. When, for example, a believer addresses God in prayer as "heavenly Father," the idea of fatherly protection and care united with the idea of a being in a space above earthly space are the symbols by which the ultimate or the infinite is present to the devotee. Likewise, when believers bathe in a sacred river, water, with its flowing and cleansing power, is a symbol of infinite spiritual harmony and cleansing.

This leads to a second important point about Tillich's understanding of symbols: a religious symbol always contains a fusion of something concrete and finite, or something taken from the world, and the infinite or the ultimate that manifests itself through it. Imaging God as a human being is incredibly common in virtually all religious traditions. This is because human beings and human lives are the richest and fullest realities of which we are aware. However, ultimacy or infinity do not only come through the image of God as a human. As mentioned above, there are religious traditions that regard natural features like rivers or mountains as sacred. Likewise, seasons, natural cycles, astrological bodies, plants, and animals have all been regarded as divine in certain religious traditions. As Tillich stresses, throughout human history virtually everything has been regarded as sacred and has functioned as a religious symbol at some time or other.

The theoretical reason that any and everything can become a symbol, for Tillich, is because the ground of being is in any and everything. The infinite infuses all reality. It is at the basis of all

---

[3] DF 42.

[4] ST I 239.

things. Therefore, anything can symbolize it. This is the metaphysical foundation for Tillich's conception of the operation of symbols and their universality.

A third important feature of religious symbols is that while they involve something ordinary and concrete, what they mediate is beyond the ordinary and the concrete; as such, their appearance has a special character: whatever mediates the infinite is holy.

Holiness is not itself an object. It is a quality that permeates the experience of an object that mediates the unconditioned. There is no difference between a sacred river and any other river in terms of hydrology, geology, and biology. But a sacred river mediates something infinite for devotees. As mediator of that which is the ground of being, a sacred river has a numinous or holy quality for those involved in the tradition that experience the river in a religious way.[5] Likewise, a cross is simply two pieces of wood that represent the typical form of capital punishment used by the Roman Empire in the first century. However, it is imbued with holiness by those for whom Jesus' death on the cross is experienced as a life-giving reality.

As Tillich points out, the meaning of holiness is that which is separate, or "apart from the ordinary realm of things and experiences."[6] He commonly refers to the work of the philosopher of religion Rudolph Otto, and Otto's analysis of holiness as involving both an attractive or fascinating aspect and a fearful or even repellent aspect.[7] Humans are attracted to the holy because the infinite that is present in and through holy objects is the ground and unity

---

[5] For Tillich, a symbol can only mediate the divine if approached in the proper subjective way. He describes the subjective approach required as "ultimate concern." It is explained in the third section of this chapter.

[6] DF 14.

[7] Rudolph Otto's work, *The Idea of the Holy* (Oxford University Press, 1958) was first published in German in 1917. Places where Tillich mentions it include ST I 215-216; DF 13.

of all life and all meaning. At the same time, what is present in the experience of the holy is infinite and absolute, something for which we have no concepts. It repels with its greatness. The biblical literature, the foundational literature of other religions, and the experiential testimony in the literature of virtually all religious traditions testify to the experience of holiness as a vital religious element.

How does something become holy? This is a complicated question that has to do with a theory of revelation, but most generally, Tillich says, it simply happens or it does not happen. There is no rule determining whether or not something will become holy. One cannot intentionally designate an object as holy. Religious symbols cannot be manipulated and produced in this way.[8] They are born usually through the ecstatic experience of an individual.[9] They live as long as groups of people continue to experience the ultimate through them. They die when people no longer have this experience. Human history is filled with dead religious symbols and living religious traditions with their still effective symbols.

2. Patterns in the History of Religion

What I have described thus far in analyzing religious symbols is what Tillich calls the "sacramental type" or "sacramental basis" of religion.[10] All religious traditions maintain something of this sacramental basis. They value holy objects and acts through which the ultimate is manifest. However, in taking a long view of history

[8] DF 43.

[9] Ecstasy means standing outside one's ordinary self. Revelatory experiences require this special subjective condition because one is confronting that which is beyond all concepts or any ordinary state of consciousness that involves the subject grasping objects.

[10] DF 58-59; CE 58.

one can see that religious traditions have not always been stable and unchanging. Traditions are born and they can die. Certain traditions have come out of others and they maintain elements in common with the older tradition even while they add distinctive beliefs and practices. Christian history displays unhealed fragmentation with the Orthodox, Roman Catholic, and Protestant branches, with significant divides among the Protestants themselves. Can one account for the dynamics of this differentiation on some theoretical level?

Accounting for the dynamics of religious diversity is an enormously complicated issue because religious diversity is connected with the endlessly complicated details of lived human history. Lived human history involves the birth, growth, and development of numerous cultures with a variety of political, economic, social, and religious systems that interact in complex ways with other cultures. Tillich regards it as a form of hubris to think one could systematically account for the directions in all historical transitions of religious diversity. At the same time, he thinks there are common patterns or types of religious expression that can be systematically analyzed and explained.[11]

His theory explaining these patterns begins with what we have described as the sacramental basis of religion. Wherever there have been human societies, there have been religious traditions because people have experienced the infinite through symbolic objects and acts related to those objects. However, the fact remains that a sacred object is in an important sense simply an object. As such, it is always open to the possibility that it may lose its symbolic power and become just another thing.[12]

---

[11] Tillich articulated the typological patterns of religion in multiple places in his work. For important examples, see PR 88-97; ST I 218-230; DF 55-73; CE 58-59; FR 86-87.

[12] In Tillich's work, the sacramental basis of religion contains significant variety. On the one hand, there is the experience of the Divine in all

Certainly the death of religious symbols and, with that, a religious tradition itself, can and may happen through the imposition of oppressive power. A group of people may be conquered and forced to assimilate with that assimilation involving the requirement of abandoning their religious tradition for that of their conquerors. However, according to Tillich, this is not the only way religious traditions may change or die. There can also be an internal religious critique. Elements within a religious tradition might negate or critique commonly accepted religious symbols as no longer being effective mediators of the Divine presence and power. Tillich points to two major structural directions in the inner-religious critique of symbols that are historically and religiously important: the mystical and the moral.

The mystical critique seeks to go beyond the outward symbolic forms of the religious to experience a direct relation with the divine in the depths of the human self. As Tillich points out, very often this mystical tendency does not necessarily seek to eradicate or radically critique the sacramental forms of a religion. Instead, it diminishes the importance of those forms for the sake of a direct experience within. This is why there are mystical strains in the major historic monotheisms of Judaism, Christianity, and Islam, as well as in Eastern traditions, that exist alongside sacramental elements of the tradition without serious conflict.

Mystical traditions contain a tremendous variety of practices, including especially different forms of meditation or contemplation. There is variety within these traditions about the character

---

things in a non-discriminating way. This is the outlook sometimes called animism. On the other hand, there is the abstraction of the Divine from the world of objects. In this latter position, things in the world become things while the Deity is symbolized as a single being of overwhelming power, usually imaged after a male ruler. This is the position of monotheism. Tillich articulates a variety of polytheistic positions in between. See ST I 218-230.

of the mystical experience and its goal, especially whether it involves an experience of complete unity with the divine that negates individuality or unity in which individuality is nevertheless maintained. Tillich has very little to say about this variety, being content to acknowledge mysticism as a type of religious directedness that critiques symbolic form without necessarily abandoning it for the sake of direct communion with the divine.

The moral critique, in Tillich's analysis, tends to make a harsher judgment of sacramental religious forms. It accuses the religious symbols of becoming demonic or heteronomous, confusing themselves with that which they are supposed to represent. For those imbued with the moral religious directedness, God is not pleased with the correct worship in the traditional form overseen by supposed religious experts. The latter are simply trying to manipulate and control the uncontrollable God with their religious cult. What God wants is not for the faithful to follow the rules for correct worship, but for the faithful to live in the right way.

Tillich sometimes calls this religious direction the holy as "what ought to be."[13] The infinite infuses everything, including our moral directedness. It can become a place of immediate religious awareness. When this happens, moral laws are the laws of God.

Famous examples of the moral critique for Tillich include the Hebrew prophets' critique of the Priestly system of sacrifice and the Protestant critique of the Roman Catholic sacramental system. While the moral critique may negate some symbols, it cannot rid itself of all symbols. It may involve the reinterpretation of symbols, as is the case with the Protestant reinterpretation of the Roman sacramental system. If it eradicated all symbols, however, it would lose its religious basis. As Tillich points out, there is always

[13] DF 56; CE 58.

something of this danger at the basis of the moral critique. Because the moral critique negates some sacramental reality for the sake of right action, it can potentially drain all sacramental reality and transform itself into a purely autonomous situation. As a liberal Protestant himself, Tillich recognized that liberal Protestantism always faces the danger. It may become an ethical club that loses its religious basis.

Tillich emphasizes that the sacramental basis of religion, the mystical tendency, and the moral tendency are types or directions concrete religious traditions take. No particular tradition ever fully embodies a type. It is, rather, a matter of emphasis with certain traditions leaning toward one type or another while assimilating elements of all the types in some way.

3. The Religious Orientation

Famously, Tillich defined the religious orientation of the human subject as "ultimate concern." The term "concern" is a comprehensive term intentionally chosen to express the human relation to all aspects of reality. To be concerned is to care about something. Except perhaps in cases of extreme depression or listlessness, we care about all things in all directions of life. We have material concerns, like those for food, shelter, and clothing because we are finite material beings. On another level, we have economic concerns about whether we have the right system to provide food, shelter, clothing, and other material goods for ourselves and others. We have moral concerns about whether we treat others correctly and whether we are treated correctly. We have social justice concerns about whether we organize and operate society to be fair to everyone in it. We have vocational concerns about finding meaningful work. We are concerned with finding truth individually and collectively in the sciences. We are concerned with aesthetic expression as well as relaxation and entertainment. Again, this broad term encompasses all directions of human life and human fulfillment.

When Tillich uses the modifier "ultimate" to describe the religious concern, he means the religious concern is the deepest and most profound of our concerns. It is the human concern with infinite or limitless significance. At one point Tillich describes it as a concern that "determines our being or not-being."[14] Ultimate meaning is at stake in this concern. In this sense, it is the most existential of our concerns. The fulfillment of the deepest meaning of life, the telos or goal of life, hinges upon this concern.

An individual or particular concern in which ultimate meaning is at stake would have to express itself as a person's highest concern. It is the concern that takes precedence over all other concerns. If push comes to shove, it could insist that all other concerns be sacrificed for it. At the same time, a concern about ultimate meaning has to involve some vision of ultimate fulfillment. Ultimate meaning is to be found in this realization. The goal of life hinges upon directing one's life with limitless passion toward the realization of this concern. Tillich expresses this by saying an ultimate concern promises "ultimate fulfillment."[15] It expresses this promise through symbols of completed bliss, like the symbols of heaven, nirvana, or moksha. The back side of such a promise is missing out on ultimate fulfillment if one does not orient one's life in the direction demanded by the concern.

One of the important features of Tillich's analysis of ultimate concern is his claim that any human concern can become an ultimate concern for an individual or group. Tillich lived through the emergence of National Socialism in Germany. He saw some of his fellow citizens make the greatness of the German state and the

[14] ST I 14.

[15] DF 2-3.

Aryan people their ultimate concern. They were willing to sacrifice everything for the State and ultimate fulfillment was envisioned with the coming thousand-year reign of the Third Reich. For Tillich, to comprehend this emergent nationalism required analysis with religious categories.

Because the ultimate or infinite pervades everything and because ultimate meaning is at the basis of all human activity, anything can become an object of ultimate concern. Besides the State, Tillich stresses that economic success is an ultimate concern for some people in the West. It was true in his time and still is the case in our time that there are those who are not satisfied with trying to find a meaningful job in which they make enough money to live a full and satisfying life. Instead, they want to rise to the top in a competitive economic system, make more money than they could ever spend, and wield power, influence and recognition for being at the top even if that means sacrificing other concerns like health, family life, friendships, and creative leisure interests.

We could update and add to Tillich's list of possible objects of ultimate concern. For some people, their ultimate concern may be achieving social justice, which they are willing to work for endlessly. Ultimate fulfillment lies in a just society where equality prevails and the vision or promise of this society keeps them tirelessly working toward it. Environmentalists may find their ultimate concern in protecting biodiversity. Ultimate fulfillment lies in a future where human impact is limited and sustainable, and there is secure protection for the diversity of species of life on earth. For others still, ultimate fulfillment could come in sports, aesthetic expression, popularity, or seeking pleasure of various kinds. Adventure, travel, and the constant stimulation of seeing new sights could be one's core vision of fulfillment.

One of Tillich's points about ultimate concerns is that they manifest themselves in people's lives in a complex way. Tillich uses passive language to describe the emergence of an ultimate concern in someone's life. People are "grasped by" an ultimate concern.[16] In other words, it is not that an individual goes about seeking an object of ultimate concern, and, confronted with an array of options like those listed above, the person one day decides to make one of the options their ultimate concern. Certainly a person's will is involved, but holding an ultimate concern is much more complicated than one day reaching out and making a choice. One's entire life trajectory and all of the influences on it, as well as unconscious desires, are all involved in the determination of an ultimate concern. Given the distinctive character, outlook, and abilities of any individual, along with their time and place in history and the distinctive social context and array of influences and opportunities that context provides, an ultimate concern of a certain kind takes hold in someone's life.

All of the things listed above as possible objects of ultimate concern, including the State and one's economic condition, have a legitimate standing in human life. In Tillich's analysis, the question is not whether these things have a legitimate standing in life but whether they can rightly stand as the object of a limitless concern, or a concern about one's being or not being. His claim is that ordinary finite concerns cannot rightly have this role. They are inadequate vehicles for ultimate fulfillment. When they take over someone's life as an ultimate concern, rather than fulfilling that life, they invariably limit it and close it down in some way or ways. Although he does not use this term explicitly, they are secular idols. Having become secular idols, in Tillich's categories, they are demonic. Ultimately, they destroy the self or limit aspects of it, instead of fulfilling the self. This may sound relatively innocuous, but often it is not the case in the real world as the example of the German State and the Aryan people becoming an object of ultimate concern shows. The realm of ultimate concern is a realm of

[16] CE 4.

potential fulfillment and vivid conflict because ultimate meaning is at stake in every ultimate concern, making the realm of ultimate concern the realm of limitless passion.

The fact that anything can be an ultimate concern has important implications for Tillich's understanding of God. God is not an existing thing alongside the universe. God is the infinite that infuses all finite reality including all directions of human life and human meaning. In religion, God is grasped immediately through symbols. In order for the subject to grasp the ultimate through a symbol, they must be in a state of ultimate concern. Without that state, the symbol is just another object. A sacred mountain is just a mountain; an image of the Deity is simply the image of a person. Ultimacy in the subject in the form of an ultimate concern must exist in correlation to the ultimacy experienced through a religious symbol in every religious experience.

In Tillich's analysis, ultimate concerns are universal.[17] Everyone has one. Because of this, religion is universal. If a secular object is one's ultimate concern, that object is a religious symbol mediating ultimacy for the person who has it as their ultimate concern. Put differently, that object is a manifestation of God to that person. This is why Tillich denies that atheism can be an authentic position for anyone. Someone may claim to be an atheist theoretically, but insofar as an ultimate concern is manifest in their lives, their lives reveal ultimacy or God.

While there are secular ultimate concerns, it is in the realm of what we call religion where ultimate concerns are most commonly manifest. The Deity is the object of ultimate concern. However, no Deity is simply an abstract object of devotion. Gods reveal themselves and in so doing they evidence particular characteristics and often give instructions and directions. Gods may explain how, where and when they are to be worshipped. They may

---

[17] TC 3-9.

give instructions for how society is to be organized, and directions about right beliefs versus wrong beliefs, and right actions versus wrong actions. All of these things are imbued with ultimate meaning in a religious tradition oriented around this deity.

Because Divine revelations are concrete, there is always the chance that what Tillich calls heteronomy or the demonic can take hold in religion as well. A God can reveal something that turns out to be destructive for the subject rather than fulfilling for it. In the final analysis, a true object of an ultimate concern must be concrete but not heteronomous. A relation to this object has to both integrate and fulfill the subject. The ultimacy manifest in the object of one's ultimate concern must take up and fulfill all other finite concerns rather than negating them or elevating certain forms to demonic status.

Chapter 6

God and Culture

Culture is a complex concept because it refers to the totality of distinctive ways a group of people express their relationship to each other and to the world. These ways take shape over the course of generations and become the unspoken fabric of life for a group of people. Certainly, the way material needs like food, shelter, and clothing are met is part of culture. The spices used in cooking, the design of casual and formal clothing, and the subtlety of architectural details all bespeak of distinctive cultural patterns. But culture also involves deeper meanings. It involves the organizational patterns of a group of people and these patterns include the expressed or implied values of a group. Does the group allow and even expect individuals to find their own way in the world as much as possible or do the demands of the collective determine the role of most people? How do the different generations treat each other? Is it youth or old age that is primarily revered? What role does gender play in expectations regarding vocation and social interaction? How are the different kinds of work rewarded? Who holds power or authority in family life and larger social groups and how do they wield that power? All of these things are aspects of culture and all of them involve values.

Tillich was concerned with the phenomenon of culture throughout his career. This concern certainly involved the way culture and religion relate to each other, but it also involved what he regarded as the religious aspect of culture. Tillich's interpretation of culture as involving religious meaning is an important contribution of his thought. Using his own vocabulary, this aspect of his thought is often called the "theology of culture."[1] This chapter is focused on this aspect of Tillich's thought because it is important for a complete understanding of Tillich's idea of God. For Tillich, God is to be found not just in the religious realm, but in culture.

1. The Religious Depth of Culture

The previous chapter included a description of ultimate concern and emphasized Tillich's claim that anything can become a matter of ultimate concern. We could put this in a different way and say that any cultural phenomenon, like material concerns or economic success, can take on an explicitly religious meaning. Usually cultural phenomena are considered matters of preliminary concern. When they become ultimate concerns, they are religious symbols mediating what is taken to be ultimate. They express one's vision or ideal of ultimate fulfillment. In this analysis of Tillich's, cultural phenomena are interpreted as explicitly religious. While this is one of Tillich's important insights about religion and culture, it is also the case for him that cultural phenomena themselves always embody an implicitly religious meaning. Put differently, the ultimacy that is directly intended in religious activity is also always present in cultural activity. It is not directly intended but indirectly involved.

---

[1] One of Tillich's earliest publications is from a lecture he gave in 1919 called "On the Idea of a Theology of Culture." It is translated and reprinted in *What is Religion?* (Harper and Row, 1969).

To understand how this is the case we first need to recall that for Tillich cultural acts are acts of meaning. The human realm is distinct from other realms because in it the relatedness to reality is elevated from an expression of given laws or instincts to an expression of meaning. To realize meaning presupposes freedom, full self-awareness, and the capacity to grasp and understand reality in universal concepts. With these capacities, realizing meaning involves entering the realm of values, rather than merely being subject to given aspects of reality. As humans, we do not just live by sets of laws ingrained into the universe. We live by values and norms. We say it is good to live this way rather than that way. It is good to provide children with education and allow them to choose their own vocation. It is good for women to have career opportunities equal to those of men and young girls should be encouraged to find and develop their unique abilities. It is good that rich and poor alike be treated equally under the law. It is good for children to respect the elderly. It is good for people to develop an appreciation of beauty in nature and in the human creations of art, music, and literature. It is good to have meaningful work and to take time off of work for meaningful leisure. All of these things and so much more are the norms of culture or the norms of meaningful human life. Human cultural life is life in meanings or life in norms.

As Tillich points out, these norms are not merely discovered by humans. They are created. All of human life and human history is, in this fundamental sense, creative.[2] We create the norms by which we live and each culture is a distinct compilation and combination of the norms of life. We also constantly adapt these

[2] The creative character of human life was a constant theme in Tillich's work. It is prominent in his first book-length work, *The System of the Sciences according to Objects and Methods* (see, for example, SS 137-145). It plays a major role throughout his *Systematic Theology* (see, for example, ST I 77-79 and ST III 30-106).

norms over time as cultures engage in internal critique and transformation, and as they come into contact with one another.

For Tillich, cultural norms are not created out of nothing. They are rooted in being or being-itself. Being-itself has the capacity to realize the variety of norm-giving cultures that exist and that have existed throughout history. This is why Tillich calls being-itself, or the ground of being, also the ground of meaning. The infinite that is God permeates everything. In the human sphere, it manifests in religion where God or the infinite is experienced directly through symbols. It also manifests in culture, where God or the infinite is the basis of the realm of meaning in which we live.

Tillich is not a blind and naïve optimist who overlooks the problematic aspects of culture and human history in general. He lived through too much devastation in the two World Wars of the twentieth century to embrace such a view. He affirms that cultures are not only rooted in being-itself, but are also always in some sense estranged from that rootedness. They develop destructive rather than fulfilling creations and they engage in destructive relations with each other. All of this makes up the complicated dynamics of history and the problematic nature of cultural oppression, war, and violence. All of this should not be overlooked from a Tillichean point of view. However, the basis of these problematic aspects of culture must be understood from a perspective that grasps the rootedness of culture in being-itself. Tillich says at one point, "the negative lives from the positive."[3] The negative is always the perversion, distortion, or lack of what should be a right realization of meaning. Beneath the negative is a positive structure that is rooted in being-itself, the ground of all reality. The negative is recognizable only as a breach or break from a positive structure that it violates.

---

[3] CB 176.

2. The Formal Structure of Culture

Tillich proposes an understanding of the foundational structure of culture and, with this, a grasp of the different directions in which the unconditioned or the infinite is present within culture.[4] He derives this foundational structure from two bases: 1) the two-fold structure of human life, and 2) the two-fold structure of experienced reality.

First, human life involves an endless alteration and unity between taking in reality and inserting oneself into reality. Tillich refers to these two aspects of life as the ability "to grasp and to shape reality."[5] We perceive the world through our senses and try to understand it. We are, however, also always part of the world that we perceive and try to understand. Based on our taking in of the world, we insert ourselves into the world in distinctive ways, and thereby shape the world.

It is Tillich's claim that while all of life is an endless alteration and unity between the elements of grasping and shaping, one or the other element predominates in certain directions of life. For example, when we are contemplative, the element of grasping predominates. In building a skyscraper, the element of shaping predominates. While neither grasping nor shaping can live without the other (one has to develop plans to build a skyscraper and one has to set aside an area for contemplation), in certain directions of life, one or the other element comes to the fore.

Second, the reality we experience in our grasping and shaping contains both a formal, ordered, or structured element, and a dynamic, expressive element. We grasp things through universal

---

[4] This structure is present through the entirety of Tillich's thought. It is prominent in his first book-length work *The System of Sciences According to Objects and Methods* (see, for example, SS 175-203) and his mature *Systematic Theology* (see, for example, ST I 75-80).

[5] ST I 75.

concepts by their form. We would not know what something is if it did not have a form. We recognize plants, animals, minerals, and human productions on the micro and macro scale by grasping the form of things. But things are never merely their form. In and through the form there is vividness, color, life, or elements of dynamic expressivity. Animals are not simply bland instances of a species. They evoke wonder and mystery with their way of being in the world. Likewise, a mountain or a lake are not simply geographical features that we can define through using the proper concepts. They express beauty, grandeur, and serenity. Reality is ordered and reality is expressive. Tillich's thought accounts for both elements.[6]

The two-fold structure of the human relation to reality and the two-fold structure of experienced reality can be combined to establish the foundational elements of culture. When the grasping of reality predominates, it can be directed either to the form of reality or to its expressive character. What we call knowing is the grasping of reality directed to form. Art is the taking in of reality directed to its expressive character. In our time, we have in the developed Western world the rigorous forms of knowing in the sciences, but we also have other ways of transmitting knowledge. Examples of the latter include the transmission of information from parent to child, or craftsperson to apprentice. Every culture throughout history has survived on the basis of being able to gather new knowledge and transmit it through the generations. And every human culture develops art. This includes, in our time, music, the visual arts, drama, literature, and film.

---

[6] In Tillich's early German work, he distinguished between three elements: form, content (inhalt) and import (gehalt). Everything has a form. Form is always the shaping of some content. Form and content together have expressivity and vividness. They have import (gehalt). See, for example, SS 33-37.

When the insertion of oneself into reality predominates, it too can be directed either to the form of reality or to its expressive character. The directedness to form yields the systems of law, order, and justice that determine our relations with one another. The directedness to the expressive character of reality yields the variety of forms of community or communal relations.

All societies live through the development of systems of justice, whether these are written formal systems like our contemporary Western systems, or oral traditions. It is also the case that every society structures itself communally and embraces various forms of family life, clan life, urban life, rural life, and national identities. These communal forms are not necessarily written down or established by strict formal laws of justice (although all communal forms must follow the laws of justice). In that sense, they lean more toward the expressive character of reality.

For Tillich, communal life involves relations of love, with love being defined in the widest sense as that which unites or binds people to each other. There is erotic love in a marriage relationship, and there is familial love among people who share a family background. More broadly, there is the love of one's place and people, there is the love of one's nation and its inhabitants, and there is the love of humanity or the binding connection to all people on the planet. In the human insertion into reality in which our relationships with each other are established, we develop both the formal laws of justice and the expressive character of loving communities.

This analysis of the foundational structure of culture does not include every element of cultural life. It de-emphasizes the material, technical, and vocational elements of culture. Tillich's focus, instead, is on what could be called the spiritual aspects of culture, or those aspects that are most directly related to meaningful norms.

Being-itself or meaning-itself lies at the basis of each aspect of culture Tillich articulates. The basis of knowledge is truth-itself. The basis of art is beauty-itself. The basis of law is justice-itself. The basis of community is love-itself. All are expressions of being-itself that become manifest in the different directions of human activity.[7]

3. Being-Itself in Culture as Presence and Demand

I have repeatedly stressed that for Tillich, being-itself is not a thing. It is infinity or ultimacy that manifests itself in and through things. In this analysis of culture, being-itself manifests through the finite realizations of the directions of culture. In Tillich's analysis, the appearance of being-itself in cultural products unites presence and demand.[8] Being-itself is manifest in cultural products as a present reality or an accompanying element. At the same time, what is experienced in the presence of being-itself is experienced as infinite and ultimate, and therefore never exhausted by any finite cultural form. The inexhaustibility of being-itself working in the subject and through cultural forms generates a demand for new forms.

---

[7] ST I 79-80.

[8] This is a constant theme in Tillich's thought. He expresses it clearly in his early work on the philosophy of religion where he claims there are three elements in every conscious act of meaning: 1) A context of meaning in which each individual realization of meaning stands; 2) The unconditioned meaning that gives meaningfulness to every meaning; and 3) A demand to fulfill the unconditioned meaning (PR 56-59).

The manifestation of the unconditioned as presence and demand can be shown in any of the directions of culture, although it is perhaps most easily explained by referring to the realm of art. In any great work of music, for example, there is the manifestation of something infinite or ultimate through the finite form. This is why great works of music are called great and speak to audiences through the generations. They can be played again and again and never be exhausted. Something of infinite beauty or expressiveness, of beauty-itself, realizes itself through the finite form. The finite form involves the instruments and their combination along with the particular musical notation creating melodic and harmonic structures that express the style of a particular era.

While beauty-itself is realized through the finite form, it is always inexhaustible. No composer, no matter how great, could ever claim to finish or complete the totality of music in some composition or even in the series of compositions that composer produces in his or her lifetime. It would be absurd to think that music-itself could ever be finished. In this sense, the unconditioned appears not only as presence in a musical composition but as demand. Every composition contains the demand for more compositions, further creativity, and further expressivity.

What is true for music is true for all art, and all directions of cultural activity. The unconditioned manifests as presence and demand in the arenas of knowledge, art, justice, and love. Every piece of knowledge, every enactment of justice, and every realization of love contains within it something infinite. At the same time, our knowledge will never be complete, justice never fully realized, and love never exhausted in any communal expression of it. Cultural life is and always must be dynamic because it contains within itself the infinite demand for further, greater, better, and ever more expressive realizations.

Tillich claims that if humans ever lost sight of the unconditioned demand in the arenas of cultural life, we would become merely crafty animals. We would be savvy creatures with big brains who know how to use tools effectively to procure goods for ourselves. We could provide food, shelter, and clothing for ourselves, but we would lose touch with the depth of meaning and, as such, our lives would be drained of meaning. We would lose what makes us human.

The term Tillich uses to describe the human being is "spirit." He defines spirit as a "unity of power and meaning."[9] Power, for Tillich, is most basically self-actualization and what humans actualize is a life under meaningful norms, or the ongoing life of culture.

The God that is manifest in culture is the same God that is manifest in religion. This God is not known directly and immediately through religious symbols but indirectly and in a mediated way through cultural products. The danger of culture is that it may lose sight of its foundation in God or being-itself. When it does, it makes God distant and irrelevant while culture itself becomes shallow or subject to irrational or arbitrary norms.

For Tillich, religion is required to establish the rootedness in being-itself from which culture can become unhinged. Religion is the direct relation to being-itself. Being-itself is the unity and source of all meaningfulness. When culture threatens to lose this unity and perhaps spin out of control, it should be religion that recenters culture, heals it, and brings it back to its harmony in its groundedness in being-itself.

Religion, however, always faces its own danger vis-à-vis culture. Its danger is that it would dictate to culture, telling culture what must count as knowledge, art, justice, and love because it presumes to know what God says is knowledge, art, justice, and

[9] ST III 22.

love. Religion must be able to guide and heal culture by keeping it open to its unity with being-itself without threatening cultural autonomy. Religion opens culture to its depths while culture insists that religion give it sway in its legitimate realm and not impose upon it. When this occurs, as explained in chapter three, theonomy emerges.

Conclusion

Who or what is God? In many ways this appears to be an easy question, unworthy of a book length treatise. In a monotheistically imbued culture, God is conceived as a supernatural being with defined attributes like eternality, omnipotence, omniscience, and complete goodness. God is envisioned as "out there." The only meaningful question is whether this God, who is encapsulated in a mental concept, really exists outside the mind or is merely a projection of the mind.

Paul Tillich worked tirelessly to break down this understanding of God and the God-world relation. For Tillich, God is not a distinct substance with attributes. God is infinity, absoluteness, or unconditionality, and these unavoidably abstract yet expressive terms are not concepts of an object. And God is not "out there." God is "through here." Infinity and absoluteness do not refer to a separate thing, but to the infinite depth within things.

In Tillich's vision, being-itself pervades all natural objects, giving them their majesty, dignity, and greatness, so that no thing is ever merely a thing. God is in the depths of nature. In the darting of a rabbit across a field, the form of the tiniest structures visible under a microscope, the austere ruggedness of a desert landscape, or the mysterious glow of nebula in the night sky, a depth is present that makes it great.

In Tillich's vision, God is in the depths of culture. In the striving for knowledge, the expressivity of art, the systems of justice, and the bonding forms of community, an infinite depth appears both as presence and demand. The presence gives cultural products their meaningful depth. Knowledge is not merely for power over things and others. Knowing has dignity. To gain a new insight into the natural world, human history, or the character of lived reality fills with satisfaction. But no new insight, however revolutionary, ever completes our knowledge. A drive for more whose basis is infinite remains. The dignity of others is immediately given in our relations with them, and our systems of justice are meant to protect and express this inherent depth of dignity. We stand when a judge enters the courtroom not for the individual judge but for the infinitely meaningful reality of justice in our relationships that the judge represents. Yet no system of justice is ever perfect or ever complete. The demand for perfection and completion continues to permeate every legal act and every legal ruling.

While our cultural life is pervaded in all directions with infinite meaning, in Tillich's vision, it is in religion where this meaning is experienced most directly, even while, paradoxically, it is here that this expression takes symbolic form. In religion, a concrete object mediates the unconditioned, which is both in and beyond it, in a direct way. For those who approach the religious object with an attitude of ultimate concern, real ultimacy is manifest and experienced. At the same time, the object remains an object within the world of objects. Bread is still bread. Wine is still wine. No object is ever adequate to the fullness of infinity it manifests.

After describing the evolution of myriad biological species from simpler forms in *The Origin of Species*, Charles Darwin famously claimed, "There is grandeur in this view of life..." Certainly the same must be said of Tillich's view of natural, cultural, and religious life. There is grandeur in his vision. Culture is not cut off from ultimate meaning but pervaded with it. As Tillich himself pointed out, the very experience of meaninglessness, however fraught with pain for those caught in its grip, presupposes a connection to the ground of meaning.[1] Without this connection, the experience of meaninglessness is not possible. With this connection, there ever arises the possibility of the creation of concrete cultural and religious forms filled with meaning. In Tillich's vision, religion is not a childish thing to be left behind as culture becomes autonomous. Neither does religion involve willing oneself to believe something that is unbelievable through some magical, desperate, or stubborn act of faith. Religion is the place where the ultimate touches life most directly. Because of this, it is the place of life's deepest meaning and the place fraught with the greatest danger of misunderstanding and potential destructiveness.

There is grandeur in this view of life, but why is it not more widely accepted? It is complicated to think about something that is ultimate reality itself, but that cannot be grasped by the mind and determined as a separate object. To embrace Tillich's view of life requires seeing the world and God not as a series of blocked and isolated things that are merely externally related to each other. It requires seeing all things, including the natural world and human culture, as being open to powers that pour through them like sunlight through the stained glass windows of a cathedral. This view of life does not contradict the isolating and separating approach to reality that is characteristic of much of the sciences, but it does limit that approach to one sphere, one kind of insight.

There is grandeur in this view of life, but is it true? Is it veridical? In responding to this question, Tillich consistently pointed to the indubitable character of the experience of ultimacy

[1] Tillich makes this argument on the basis of a larger and more complex historical and theoretical analysis at the end of CB. See 182-190.

in life. What is unconditioned cannot be grasped and controlled, but it is there as presence, power, and demand if you open to it and look for it. Something ultimate is experienced in and through the Bach Brandenberg Concertos, the gathering of volunteers for an annual bird count on a river, a parent teaching a child how to grow vegetables, and the reading of the Torah portion in a synagogue. Ultimacy is present in life. Look for it and you will find it. To reduce it to something else or explain it away as something else is to deny the integrity of the experience and our capacity to understand life as it gives itself. For Tillich, life has depths and in those depths is the presence of God.

Bibliography

WORKS BY PAUL TILLICH

Christianity and the Encounter of the World Religions. New York: Columbia University Press, 1963.

The Courage to Be. New Haven and London: Yale University Press, 1952.

Dynamics of Faith. New York: Harper and Row, 1957.

The Future of Religions. New York: Harper and Row, 1966.

On the Idea of a Theology of Culture, in *What is Religion?* Translated by James Luther Adams. New York, Evanston, and London: Harper and Row, 1969.

Philosophy of Religion, in *What is Religion?* Translated by James Luther Adams. New York, Evanston, and London: Harper and Row, 1969.

The Protestant Era, abridged edition. Translated by James Luther Adams. Chicago: University of Chicago Press, 1957.

System of the Sciences according to Objects and Methods. Translated by Paul Wiebe. London and Toronto: Associated University Presses, 1981.

Systematic Theology. Three volumes. Chicago: University of Chicago Press, 1951, 1957, 1963.

Theology of Culture. London, Oxford, New York: Oxford University Press, 1959.

WORKS CITED OR REFERENCED IN THE TEXT

Anselm. *Proslogion*, in *Monologion and Proslogion*. Translated by Thomas Williams. Indianapolis: Hackett, 1996.

Aquinas, Thomas. *Summa Theologica*, I. Westminster MD: Christian Classics, 1981.

Augustine, *Earlier Writings*. Philadelphia: Westminster Press, 1953.

Bonhoeffer, Dietrich. *Letters and Papers from Prison*. Edited by Eberhard Bethge. New York: Simon and Schuster, 1997.

Bultmann, Rudolph. *New Testament and Mythology and other Basic Writings.* Translated and Edited by Schubert Ogden. Minneapolis: Fortress Press, 1984.

Dawkins, Richard. *The God Delusion*. Boston and New York: Houghton Mifflin, 2008.

Dennett, Daniel. *Breaking the Spell: Religion as a Natural Phenomenon.* New York: Viking Penguin, 2006.

Freud, Sigmund. *The Future of an Illusion*. Pacific Publishing Studio, 2010.

Gilkey, Langdon. *Gilkey on Tillich*. Oregon: Wipf and Stock, 1990.

Harris, Sam. *The End of Faith: Religion, Terror, and the Future of Reason*. New York and London: W.W. Norton, 2005.

Hitchens, Christopher. *God is not Great: How Religion Poisons Everything*. New York: Hachette Book Group, 2007.

Hume, David. *Dialogues Concerning Natural Religion*. Indianapolis: Hackett, 1980.

James, Robison. *Tillich and World Religions: Encountering other Faiths Today*. Macon Georgia: Mercer University Press, 2003.

Jefferson, Thomas. *The Jefferson Bible: The Life and Morals of Jesus of Nazareth*. Washington D.C.: Smithsonian Books, 2011.

Johnson, Elizabeth. *She Who Is: The Mystery of God in Feminist Theological Discourse*. Crossroads Publishing Company, 1992.

Kant, Immanuel. *Critique of Pure Reason*. Translated by Norman Kemp Smith. New York: St Martin's Press, 1965.

__________. *Foundations of the Metaphysics of Morals*. New York: Macmillan, 1959.

__________. *Critique of Practical Reason*. New York: Macmillan, 1956.

Lindbeck, George. *The Nature of Doctrine*. Philadelphia: Westminster Press, 1984.

Marx, Karl. *Critique of Hegel's Philosophy of Right*. Translated by Annette Jolin and Joseph O'Malley. Cambridge: Cambridge University Press, 1970.

McFague, Sallie. *Models of God: Theology for an Ecological Nuclear Age*. Minneapolis: Fortress Press, 1987.

New Interpreters Dictionary of the Bible. Vol 1. Nashville: Abingdon Press, 2006.

Nietzsche, Friedrich. *On the Genealogy of Morals*. Cranston RI: Angelnook Publishing, 2012.

Otto, Rudolph. *The Idea of the Holy*. Oxford: Oxford University Press, 1958.

Ruether, Rosemary Radford. *Sexism and God Talk: Toward a Feminist Theology*. Boston: Beacon Press, 1983.

Robinson, John A. T. *Honest to God*, Philadelphia: Westminster Press, 1963.

Scharlemann, Robert. *Reflection and Doubt in the Thought of Paul Tillich*. New Haven and London: Yale University Press, 1969.

Schleiermacher, Friedrich. *On Religion: Speeches to its Cultured Despisers*, Translated and Edited by Richard Crouter. Cambridge: Cambridge University Press, 1988.

__________. *The Christian Faith*. Edinburgh: T and T Clark, 1999.

Troeltsch, Ernst. *Religion in History*. Translated by James Luther Adams and Walter F. Bense. Minneapolis: Fortress Press, 1991.

Index